Radicle Growth

RADICLE
GROWTH

Transform into an Unstoppable Leader
through Mastering the Art of Questions

DAVE REYNOLDS

LIONCREST
PUBLISHING

RADICLE GROWTH

Transform into an Unstoppable Leader through Mastering the Art of Questions

FIRST EDITION

ISBN   978-1-5445-4819-7 *Paperback*
      978-1-5445-4820-3 *Ebook*
      978-1-5445-4712-1 *Audiobook*

This book is dedicated to my children, Oliver and
Cooper, as a reminder that anything is possible.

CONTENTS

ACKNOWLEDGMENT

I'd like to thank Pablo, my mentor for over ten years who showed me the value of asking the right questions to find the right answers.

Introduction

FINDING THE RIGHT ANSWER

BOSSES DON'T NEED THE ANSWERS IF THEY KNOW THE RIGHT QUESTIONS

"You can tell whether a man is clever by his answers. You can tell whether a man is wise by his questions."

—NAGUIB MAHFOUZ

One of the first things we do in our workshops for newly promoted managers is to ask them to think of the toughest boss they have ever had. Think of the person who pushed you the most. They had high standards and expected you to meet them. They were never satisfied with simple or vague answers. When you asked them questions, they responded with their own questions. They forced you out of your comfort zone.

Six months later, after they complete our training, we ask these managers to think about the *best* boss they ever had. Who did you learn the most from? Who stretched you the most? Who paid attention to you and seemed to care the most about your improvement? Who spurred you to improve while instilling confidence that you *would* improve? Who saw something in you that you didn't see in yourself and elevated you to that level by pushing you harder to get there? Who invested in you because they knew it was possible—even if you didn't think it was.

It doesn't take them long to identify that person. Virtually every one of our participants admits the *toughest* boss was also the *best* boss.

This realization comes to them because, over the last twenty-four weeks, they've learned that the best bosses are not the people who have the most experience or have the right answers. They aren't the leaders who shower them with praise and congratulate them for every accomplishment, large or small. Instead, these bosses were great because they demanded more of their people. There was friction, sure, but that friction is what sparked the fire, the inspiration. These bosses supported them yet held them accountable.

These bosses invited their people to not just identify problems but to find solutions to those problems. These bosses didn't have easy answers but instead compelled their team members to find answers and, through that process, grow and improve. These bosses didn't tell you what you wanted to hear. They told you what you needed to hear. This didn't always make you feel good, but it helped you grow and learn. These bosses used a care-and-candor approach; they cared enough about you to be direct with you, and in that way, you experienced transformational growth. They pushed you from the nest and told you to build your wings on the way down. It was tough sometimes, but ultimately, these were the bosses who made their team members feel like they were collaborating with their supervisor, co-creating and taking ownership in solving problems and making sure their solutions truly worked.

ASKING THE RIGHT QUESTIONS

The central goal of our Radicle Growth coaching program is to help leaders—whether they were recently promoted or have been in the role for some time—acquire the skills they need to become great coaches. In our experience, becoming a great boss is not about always having the right answers. It's about asking the right *questions* to get the *best answers*. Radicle Growth teaches leaders how to use questions to coach their team members to their own answers.

Most team members already have a solution in mind but will go to the boss's office and ask for the answer anyway. Sometimes, they are just looking for an easy route. Sometimes, they just want confirmation. In a traditional, hierarchical environment, the boss gives them an answer. It's a simple and quick one-way transaction.

And it's also highly unproductive. The next day, the team member returns with another question, then another. Over time, the boss is doing little but solving problems for others. During training, we ask audiences all the time, "How often does somebody ask you for a solution and you're busy so you just quickly give them the answer?" Everyone's hands fly up. "Okay, how many of you have found they keep coming back with the same problem, and you provide the same solution?" Again, a forest of raised hands.

The whole idea behind Radicle Growth is to turn that transactional approach into a transformational one by using a two-way conversation that changes how leaders connect. The team member is no longer merely carrying out orders but instead is working with the manager on a solution. The result is that the team member is more committed because they are addressing a problem they helped solve, which increases their confidence and productivity. As their coach, you help your team members think more independently and become less dependent on you. Team members are challenged to grow. Better solutions emerge. Productivity soars. Honesty, trust, and continuous improvement become the cornerstones of a thriving workplace.

When you have a strong coaching culture like this, you get more from your teams and people. Coaching takes new knowledge and turns it into an implementation system with more accountability and urgency. One study found that training alone increases productivity by about 22 percent, but when you adopt a coaching mentality—where employees are taught to think more for themselves and work with managers on solutions—productivity increases by a staggering 88 percent.[1] That 22 percent increase is a blip that disappears quickly from your productivity

---

1   Gerald Olivero et al., "Executive Coaching as a Transfer of Training Tool: Effects on Productivity in a Public Agency," *Public Personnel Management* 26, no. 4 (1997): 465, https://doi.org/10.1177/009102609702600403.

curve, but the 88 percent comes when you take that training and extend it out—by systematizing it and standardizing it. It becomes embedded in your mindset and your operation. Knowledge alone is not power, but the *adoption* and *application* of that knowledge certainly is. The reason that coaching is four times stronger than training is that a coach gets you to use the information you learn. Coaching takes something you know or learned and puts it into a system for your work and life. Blips of productivity are great but that increased productivity is not sustainable unless you can systematize it. Solutions are better and are effectively employed. Workers take ownership and are more accountable. It's much like having a personal trainer. If you go to the gym alone, you might work out at 60 percent intensity. But if you go to the gym with your trainer, you're likely to work at 90 percent intensity.

We call it Radicle Growth because, in botany, the radicle is the first part of a seedling to emerge from the seed during the process of germination. It is the embryonic root of the plant that grows down into the soil and eventually enables the seed to sprout above the earth. In the workplace—but also in life and relationships—Radicle Growth begins with purposeful questions from a coach to a coachee.

WHAT YOU'LL LEARN

This book is written for leaders who want to hone their coaching skills and better lead their teams to new heights. Some of you might be struggling with the unceasing questions that are part of management. You might feel caught in the middle, juggling the expectations of your own bosses while patiently nurturing your team. You may even think at times of returning to those good old days when you didn't have to manage people at all!

This book will provide some fresh strategies for you. It covers the core principles we teach in our Radicle Growth coaching program, and while it will give you many ideas about how to improve as a coach and leader, it may also be the incentive you need to enroll in our coaching program and earn certification in the techniques we use.

In our training, we ask people whether they would choose a young plant to put in the ground or a seed they could bury and nurture into a young plant. Many choose a plant because they can see whether it is struggling and needs water or fertilizer. Likewise, they can be sure that it's healthy and growing. On the other hand, when you plant a seed, its growth takes place underground. You can't see it push out the radicle; you can't see the root system spreading out. But eventually, the shoot pushes through the soil, and you have a strong healthy plant.

This is an analogy for coaching. If you want to transformatively change your behavior, you have to believe in the process. It will take some time to see the results—about ninety days to see the result of a new behavior. So, just as you must believe in the radicle process or growth—that foundational growth is occurring beneath the surface—you must commit to systematizing your coaching system. Only then will you see long-term growth.

Let's define what we mean by coach and coachee. In many cases, the coach is the boss or a supervisor, and the coachee is an employee. Sometimes the coach is a peer and not a direct supervisor. My first coach—Pablo, the man to whom I've dedicated this book—was initially my direct supervisor's boss. He's had such a huge impact on my life, not only just teaching me how to ask the right questions, but forcing me into deep self-reflection by asking the right questions. But he also became a model and a mentor and someone I looked up to. A coach is also a motivator who's not only giving coachees the recognition that they're probably striving for but also in a lot of cases pushing them and challenging them to get the best of themselves. In sports, the best coaches in the world are not just there patting their players' backs but pushing them to go as far as they possibly can.

The best version of a coach is someone who believes you can achieve more—possibly more than their coachees believe they can achieve. They see something in others that they might not even see in themselves. The coaching process is about how you transform the coachee into what the coach can see in them. It's a transformative process, and being a coach is a big responsibility and investment. What's more, having the opportunity to be a coachee for a great coach is a big opportunity. When certain players get selected by certain teams, they are excited because they get to work with that team's particular coach.

Phil Jackson is a great example. When you got selected by the Chicago Bulls, it wasn't about getting selected by the Chicago Bulls, it was about getting selected by Phil Jackson. You were going to get a chance to work with Phil Jackson. Good coaches can transform another person's life. I've coached hundreds if not thousands of people, and I know that I've had a lasting effect because I've talked to them years later and saw that the things we talked about stuck with them.

This shows the transformation a coach can create. The first question we ask when we teach Radicle Growth is, "Who benefits from you taking this course and becoming a better coach?" The answer is all the people you're going to work with over the next X number of years in your career. If you apply these skills as a good coach, think about how many lives you're going to impact, helping people become better husbands, wives, or partners and/or become better bosses and leaders—potentially becoming CEOs.

A coachee is anyone who is receiving the coaching. They are receiving information, incorporating it, acting on it, and exhibiting the new behavior they've learned. In coaching, you create a relationship and invest in someone with the goal of helping them improve. You hold them accountable for following through on their commitment to the process and to the relationship. Your coaching is designed to convince the coachee to change how they think and act.

Being a coach is much like being a father. A coach must take on that level of accountability and responsibility. Being a coach is not a check-the-box job. You have to realize the responsibility and power that comes from being an impactful coach. By learning to be a great coach, you are taking on a superpower that's going to help you accelerate your career because you've got people who support you.

Here's an example. I just met with a huge car dealership owner who owns seventy or eighty dealerships. He said that if he buys a dealership in the US and the general manager leaves, almost everybody leaves with them. The GM has so much influence that they can almost take the dealership with them when they leave. As a result, this owner understands the need to work with his GMs on a consistent basis to make sure that they're happy and engaged. He wants our Radicle Growth program to help him achieve that.

In this book, we'll contrast our collaborative, Socratic approach with traditional top-down leadership. The two are a world apart. Radicle Growth inspires coaches and leaders to embrace co-creation, learning, and follow-up. It helps you build trust and forge strong work relationships. Most of those who go through our training quickly learn that their new skills help not only on the job but also in their personal lives and relationships. You learn to listen more and to engage more closely and productively.

The book will also follow the core concepts of our training, with each chapter exploring the nature of:

DISCOVERY

What is an effective question? Why is it smart to start with broad questions and gradually become more specific? What are the goals of your session with the coachee, and how can you ensure your questions align with those goals?

SELF-AWARENESS

How aware is your coachee of the problems they are facing? Before they know where they want to go, they have to determine where they are. How can you get past their superficial, self-protective answers and find the deeper truth? Bosses who identify a problem and suggest a solution cheat their team members out of the powerful experience of developing awareness. For lasting results, don't correct them. Instead, guide them to their own epiphanies. Let them have their aha moments. You will bring long-term change versus short-term corrections.

FOCUS

What are the one or two things your team members should focus on? How can you, the coach, challenge them and use the process of comparison to help them arrive at those focus areas? In a world where people are drenched in priorities, how do we help coachees pare away their challenges so they can focus on one or two things? What's the best measurement of progress in those focus areas? Do you have focus? Are you aware of what you do that has the strongest return on your time investment?

COMMITMENT

What are some realistic timelines for the results you want? This is where Radicle Growth has taken hold and the plant stem is emerging. When your coachee realizes that you're not stopping or going away—that your commitment to them is as high or higher than their own commitment—you can truly hold them accountable. Without discipline, strong follow-up, and consistency, you lose all the outcomes—as well as the relationship you've worked so hard to establish with your coachee. Likewise, the coachee must also make a commitment to the process and how they will accomplish their own goals. This is about the coachee owning the path through a guided approach. While many people look to their coach for answers, the coachees in Radicle Growth look inside themselves to learn how. Their coach is asking a lot from them—how do you want to accomplish that goal or approach that problem?—and the answer must come from the coachee. If you can find your purpose through this coaching process, getting there won't be the hard part.

FOLLOW-UP

Many coaches falter here. Without follow-through, accountability plummets. But if the coachee understands you will follow up, accountability, learning, and productivity skyrocket. This is where recognition and reward come into play. Acknowledge their effort, even if they struggle.

SYSTEMIZATION

As James Clear, the author of *Atomic Habits*, says,

> "YOU DO NOT RISE TO THE LEVEL OF YOUR GOALS. YOU
> FALL TO THE LEVEL OF YOUR SYSTEMS. YOUR GOAL IS YOUR
> DESIRED OUTCOME. YOUR SYSTEM IS THE COLLECTION
> OF DAILY HABITS THAT WILL GET YOU THERE."[2]

So why does follow-up need to be systematized? How do you develop the discipline to succeed with follow-up? What are the nuts and bolts of a good system? How can you ensure each conversation you have with your coachee is linked back to the last conversation and forward to the next one? How do you build that chain that keeps you moving forward? This book explains how to create a coaching system that works. If we don't put this coaching approach into a system, it can't be the engine that propels continuous improvement. The system provides consistency. A seed that is watered and fertilized regularly grows into a strong plant. The system works because we don't accept excuses for being too busy not to coach. We don't accept that there are too many things that are more important. Every time we coach, it's an investment that will pay off down the road with higher efficiency, better outcomes, and better people. You have to embed it in your process, and that requires patience and persistence from both the coach and the coachee. I've had clients who, five years after training, are still using the growth habit they built through the Radicle Growth program. They've changed jobs and even industries, but the principles still work—regardless of what field you're in.

---

2   James Clear, "3–2–1: On Systems vs. Goals, Identity-Based Habits, and the Lessons of Life," *James Clear* (blog), January 2, 2020, https://jamesclear.com/3-2-1/january-2-2020.

LEADING UP, ACROSS, AND DOWN

Coaching is not just for your direct reports. You can use these coaching methods to coach up to your bosses and across to your peers. Some key questions we'll explore:

- Why is coaching across often more challenging?
- Why is it also more powerful?
- How does the power of questions help you influence more people?
- Why is coaching down not as easy as everyone thinks?

People often think that when they get a title, everyone will listen to them and look up to them. Not true. You need a system to understand how to lead people, and Radicle Growth allows you to go from being a peer to being a leader. It's more about the system than it is about the title.

Great coaching is neither an art nor a science—it's both. Skilled leaders who practice using questions can develop an innate sense of when to ask a question and what question fits the coachee and the circumstance. But there is also a neuroscientific explanation for why asking questions brings about self-awareness and the positive behavioral responses you're striving for. Science validates the effectiveness of the process we teach in this book.

THE ORIGINS OF THIS BOOK

The concepts we teach in Radicle Growth came out of my own experience as a manager in the telecommunications industry fifteen years ago. I've always been a serial entrepreneur, so after I sold my first large company, I went to the mall to get a new cell phone because I'd just turned my old one in as part of the sale. Long story short, I got to know the management at the cell phone store and they talked me into coming to work for them as a manager and trainer.

As a competitive person by nature, I quickly realized that a big part of growth and success involved coaching. But at the time, coaching was about following a rigid process of coaching logs and so forth. I felt there was a better way. I felt being a coach was like being a personal trainer; you will get better results when you work with your trainer four times a month rather than once. You build a better relationship with your trainer. You develop trust in the process. There is better follow-up and more discipline. Your workouts build off of previous sessions while also preparing you for future sessions. They are connected and drive you to your overarching goals.

I learned the rudiments of the Socratic method I used from one of the top managers at the telecommunications firm—Pablo Battaro. Pablo was actually my boss's boss, but he decided to make an investment in me. He had toured our store a few months after I started and asked if I was interested in having regular coaching sessions with him. He saw something in me that I didn't see in myself, and I quickly agreed. Pablo taught me how to ask the right questions, pushing me far past what I thought possible. He was prepared and focused for every coaching session we had, and he expected me to show up the same way. In time, I started thinking more independently for myself and soon I was coaching members of my own team the way Pablo coached me. In ten years, I went from running one store doing $500,000 a year to overseeing eighteen locations throughout eastern Canada doing $40 million in revenue. During that time, I realized that the most value I offered to the people I worked with was that coaching relationship. At one location after another, we could double or triple revenues quickly thanks to the power of coaching.

Soon, I found myself working informally in other industries. I remember sitting in a box at an NHL game and chatting with a friend's wife. She was an executive in the banking industry and confided that she was struggling to increase the productivity of her team. Without really planning to, I began asking her questions. What kind of challenges was she facing? What's one thing she would change? As the players zipped around on the ice, her problems and strategies for addressing them came into focus for her. Suddenly, she turned to me and said, "Listen, you obviously have a knack for coaching people to better performance. Why don't I pay you to come in and consult for me?" So, I did. Then her husband, who was in the mortgage business, invited me to work with his people. Then a law firm called. I began working with their associates, and every one of the lawyers I worked with went on to become a partner in the firm. Coaching became a side gig for me, and in time I could systematize the process I was using.

About this time, I read business author Jim Collins's ideas about what he called "the hedgehog concept."[3] The hedgehog concept is a Venn diagram depicting:

1. What are you deeply passionate about?
2. What you can be the best in the world at.
3. What drives your economic engine?

The center of the diagram where these three circles intersect is your core value proposition. It's the thing you do best, that does the best for you, and therefore, the thing you should focus on. For me, it was training and coaching. This eventually led me to create the Rumin8 Group, a growth consultancy. Since then, we've worked in dozens of different industries, from architecture to fintech, experiencing tenfold growth in our first five years.

WHAT THIS BOOK IS AND ISN'T

This book is not about a step-by-step process where you "do this to get this." Radicle Growth is not a blueprint. It's not a magic pill you can swallow and become successful. It's not an academic theory.

Instead, it's a proven system that anyone can pick up and use. It's a process, but more importantly, it is an approach that takes time, experience, and practice. It's not a one-and-done. It's a method for shifting your paradigm from the traditional top-down, hierarchical notion of

---

3   Jim Collins, "The Hedgehog Concept," *Jim Collins* (blog), accessed September 15, 2024, https://www.jimcollins.com/concepts/the-hedgehog-concept.html.

coaching to one where the coachee arrives at their inspiration to change and improve. It's a process that fosters stronger relationships and trust.

It also delivers incredible results. I remember one day I was working with some lawyers in one of the biggest law firms in Canada. One of the firm's partners stopped me in the hallway and asked casually about the work I was doing with the company's associates. He wasn't rude, but he was sort of blunt. "Look," he said, "you don't have a legal background. How can you coach these young lawyers? How can you expect them to make partner when you know nothing about the law?"

I smiled. Remember, talking and coaching are two of my favorite things. And I love tough questions.

"Well," I said, "the truth is that the less I know, the more I can help." I went on to explain the Radicle Growth process and how it would help the firm's lawyers be more accountable, execute at a faster cadence, record more billable hours, and bring in more clients. Now the partner was smiling. He liked the sound of that. "We do lack urgency," he admitted.

We now have over a hundred clients from eight countries working in various industries, from architecture to pharma. We frequently are asked how we can help companies when we know little about the industries they operate in. The truth is, that the less we know, the more we can help. That's because the people who are on the cusp of a breakthrough often have most of the knowledge and information they need, they are just hesitant to act on it. So we take them through a discovery process where we take out most of the information they have and spread it out before them, and get them to use the information they already have more effectively. We take what they already have and make it better. When they systematize the process, they start seeing consistent results.

When I'm coming into a new industry, I say, "Teach me what you know." I don't come in as an industry expert with a plan that all they need to do is execute. As they teach me, I'll say, "Oh, why is that important? What role does that play in your industry?" They'll say, "Oh, that's super critical," and in this way, they start to realize that there are areas where they could consistently do better. From there, we build the systems that hardwire the coaching process, and their knowledge leaps from that 22 percent blip to the ongoing 88 percent growth. It feels special because the process is customized to the person doing the training.

With the law firm, we didn't set out to make them better lawyers but instead to help them build a better legal practice with more focus on growth and accountability. For example, when we asked a focus group of associates how often they got feedback on their work, they said they only got feedback when they asked for it or did something wrong. "Interesting," I said. "How much would you value consistent feedback?" Of course, they all wanted that, which left the partners hanging their heads in shame because it helped explain one of the biggest problems—employee retention. There were other issues; in fact, our questions opened up a Pandora's box that gave the partners a reason to build a strategy. By asking questions, we were able to get senior partners to learn and commit to bringing change to one of the biggest law firms in the country.

We went on to have huge success with the law firm. We brought accountability to the ranks of lawyers, and the firm became even more profitable and noteworthy.

LEARN FOR YOURSELF

Our success with the law firm and companies from twenty other industries convinced me to write this book. Many consultants like to keep their processes and techniques private because they don't want someone else to steal them. I get it, but I also think that demonstrates a scarcity mindset. I've always had an abundance mindset. I like to share our process and journey. It's great to work with an organization that already has a set of principles and appreciation for the type of coaching we teach. Not only are those organizations open to adopting our new approach to improve their business but they are eager to adopt these principles of coaching in their private lives as spouses, parents, volunteers, and civic leaders. This training allows them to have richer conversations, stronger relationships, and an ability to work in a cross-functional way throughout an organization. For us, coaching is a choice, not a title, and you can coach people at all levels—at the peer level as well as at the leadership level. You're learning a skill set that's useful in all aspects of life and work. It's a way of influencing people's growth that is incredibly rewarding.

Here's another way to look at coaching: every conversation you have with a coachee is an investment. Your relationship is an emotional bank account, and your questions are like deposits. The more you work with them, the greater your investment becomes, and the richer this emotional bank account gets. Some investments the coach makes are more significant than others and can lead to major benefits. Other investments might be smaller, such as simple follow-ups or recognition of the coachee's work and commitment. These investments accumulate over time and give you the resources you might need as a coach when it's time to challenge or push your coachee. These investments allow you to tap into this emotional bank account; you're able to be more candid with the person because they've come to see that you care. When you build up your balance in the account, it's easier when you need to make a withdrawal, such as when you have to have a difficult conversation about performance or commitment. At some point, you might need to have a candid conversation, and you can't make a withdrawal unless you've made an investment. Visualize the bank account that's being filled. Also, picture the withdrawal; if you have no money in the bank, it's difficult to withdraw funds. You can tell people what they need to hear versus what they want to hear.

Visualize a bank account that's being filled through the investments of the coach to the coachee. Now picture when you need to make a withdrawal. If you don't have money in there, it's difficult or impossible to make a withdrawal. And that's the way that coaching works; you make investments over the long term, so the account builds and grows. When it comes time to make a withdrawal, you have such a large level of investment, that it's easier for you to withdraw some of that equity. That's why people who have strong relationships and strong equity can have tougher conversations; they care with candor, and they're candid with care. You are able to tell people what they need to hear versus what they want to hear. And that's what a transformative relationship looks like.

Every question is a key to a door, and some of those doors have never been opened. As the popular saying goes,

"IF I HAD AN HOUR TO SOLVE A PROBLEM AND MY LIFE DEPENDED ON THE SOLUTION, I WOULD SPEND THE FIRST FIFTY-FIVE MINUTES DETERMINING THE PROPER QUESTION TO ASK…FOR ONCE I KNOW THE PROPER QUESTION, I COULD SOLVE THE PROBLEM IN LESS THAN FIVE MINUTES."

CHAPTER EXERCISES

A crucial piece of the Radicle Growth approach is applying the knowledge you gain. The goal of this book and our workshops isn't to just drop information into your lap but to help you incorporate what you learn into your daily conversations. We learn how to ask great questions but that skill won't help you if you don't put it into action.

With that in mind, at the end of each chapter, I'll present some thought-provoking questions to help you apply what you learned in that chapter. Application is a decision. These questions are an opportunity for you to see Radicle Growth.

GROWTH REFLECTION QUESTIONS AND ACTIVITIES

1. Write down three reasons why being a better coach and communicator would help support your growth/development.
2. Name five people who would benefit from you becoming a better coach. Describe how they will benefit.
3. Who has been your best coach and why?

1

THE DIFFERENCE BETWEEN MANAGING AND COACHING

TRAINING, COACHING, AND FEEDBACK HELP EMPLOYEES PERFORM BETTER

"A leader takes people where they want to go. A great leader takes people where they don't necessarily want to go, but ought to be."

—ROSALYNN CARTER

In the old days, bosses were managers. Their job was to establish the strategy, assign the work, set goals for their employees, and then hold employees accountable. It was more about fear management: Do it or don't work here. They were the final authority. They yelled and insulted you if they felt you needed some extra motivation. You did what they told you, and you never asked questions because you didn't want to come across as being too big for your britches. Their word was law. Even if you said something, they ignored you. These attitudes became embedded in business culture over the course of decades, creating a sense of dependency on the boss. It certainly didn't inspire workers.

Luckily, times have changed. Bosses who bully their team members, communicate poorly, or condescend to their direct reports don't last long with most companies. Employees expect more. They want to be mentored, challenged, and supported. They crave feedback and want to help solve problems, not just carry out orders. Moreover, research shows that companies that nurture their employees with training, coaching, and feedback perform better. For starters, these companies enjoy greater productivity, fewer absences, less turnover, and little theft. According to the Global Workforce Study, disengaged employees cost US companies up to $550 billion per year in lost productivity. Meanwhile, more than half of the companies that invest in coaching report higher revenue than similar organizations that don't.

Coaching in business is still a young profession. The first book on the subject came out in 1992 when John Whitmore defined coaching as "unlocking people's potential to maximize their own performance."[4] Coaching wasn't training, and it wasn't teaching. It wasn't the transfer of knowledge. Instead, it was about cultivating an individual's ability to learn and expand their skills under the guidance of a more experienced person. What's more, coaching isn't management. Management is about tasks, processes, and standard operating procedures. Coaching is about personal development and changing a team member's mindset, behaviors, confidence, and self-assurance. While old-school bosses spurned questions while they doled out directives, coaches were more likely to pose questions to spur their teams to find answers. In the old days, a boss's credibility relied on them having all the answers. Now their credibility relies on how well they can ask questions, build relationships, and draw fresh, innovative answers from the people who report to them. This shift from telling to asking alters the dynamic between leaders and their team members. It turns from a one-way conversation of the boss giving answers to a two-way conversation, where the boss challenges

---

4   John Whitmore, *Coaching for Performance: GROWing Human Potential and Purpose: The Principles and Practice of Coaching and Leadership*, 4th ed. (Nicholas Brealey Publishing, 2009), 10.

their employee to propose a solution and then closely monitors the employee's progress toward executing that solution.

ONE-WAY VS TWO-WAY CONVERSATION

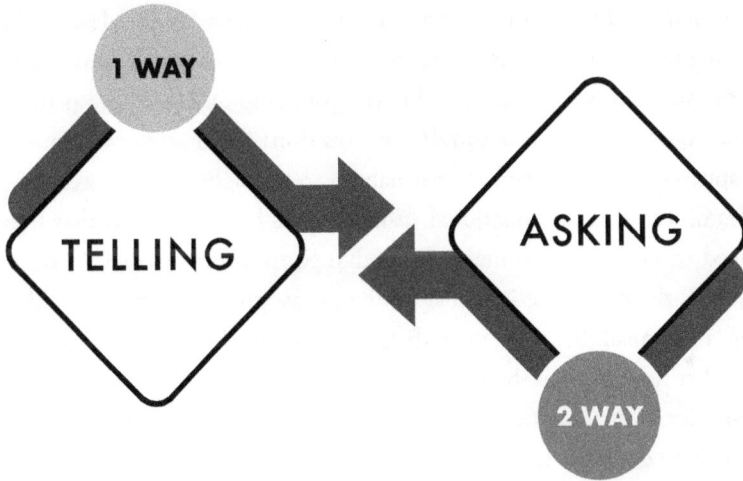

Coaching changes the boss–employee dynamic in other ways. It allows the boss to become vulnerable, and it opens their relationship with team members to broader questions, like "What do you hope to achieve?" and "What do you feel is holding you back?" It acknowledges that mentors and mentees learn together, but it also requires clear conversations about standards and accountability, which can make some employees uncomfortable. Employees quickly learn that going to the boss for an answer to a problem is no longer an option. They can go to the boss with the problem, but they are likely to be guided toward finding the answer themselves and to take responsibility for solving the problem on their own. This way, they gain confidence, new skills, and self-reliance that improves the company's bottom line and fosters continuous improvement. Remember the adage,

A DIFFERENT KIND OF WORKPLACE

The paradigm shift for leaders to unlock the superpower in their role through coaching is driven by a changing workplace. Today's leaders are trying to find more areas where they can increase a sense of "ownership" from their employees. Getting buy-in from employees empowers them and increases their accountability. You don't see that empowerment happen when the leader is merely handing out assignments and assigning deadlines. That's transactional. What leaders have learned is that they need to find a way to make the exchange transformational. In other words, the employee isn't just taking an assignment, they are taking on a responsibility with outright gusto and full-fledged commitment. Leaders have to learn their team members' passions, understanding, and capacity so they can transform the work over to them and feel confident it will be done the right way.

A byword of the modern workplace is "co-creation." That process is built on a Socratic philosophy, where the leader asks compelling questions, and the team members' response, their answer, contributes to the strategy. The coach guides the approach with this collaborative question-and-answer method, bringing about more ownership on the team member's part.

Having a great coach with whom you meet regularly is like having a personal trainer. Are you going to get in better shape working out occasionally on your own or working out on a regular schedule under the tutelage of a skilled mentor? Training on a schedule with guidance brings big improvements because you greatly expand your input on what gives you the strongest output.

Using questions as a guide to bring your team members to strong answers gets them off the beaten path between so-called "bosses" and "workers." The questions help them think differently and bring them to a different destination. You're not manipulating them but you are helping them transition to better self-awareness and self-actualization. They're encouraged to reflect on current information differently, so you're giving them a different code. The hardest part of this process is that as the leader, you might know in the first two minutes of a conversation what they need to do from a strategy perspective, but you must spend the time needed to help them realize what they need to do. That may sound a little tedious and perhaps not the best use of time, but it isn't useless. This process is about making it their idea, not yours, to create ownership and accountability. It's actually an efficient use of time because the person you're coaching will come away with more ownership, accountability, and commitment, and they'll go about their work with more passion. In the long run, that extra time prevents having the same conversations about the same problems over and over because the team members better understand the solution and learn to apply that confident, solution-oriented approach to future issues. As Stephen Covey notes in his book *The 7 Habits of Highly Effective People*, the only way to be efficient in conversations with others is to take your time. "With people, fast is slow, and slow is fast."[5] Take your time.

"I can't believe I haven't thought about that before," your coachee will say. They'll share their experience with their peers, and in that way, a culture of coaching spreads through your team and your company. Moreover, the coach enjoys a sense of pride in seeing a team member solve a problem and own an idea as theirs and not just another directive from the boss. They've helped light the path with their questions.

Patience is the greatest skill in this process. We live in a rush-rush world, and it's tempting to cut the talk, state the answer, and send the team member on their way to execute. But how many times will they come back to ask for clarification? How committed will they be to carry out the solution? How quickly and how focused will they be on the task? With coaching, patience helps clarify things and builds a compelling commitment in your team members. They can't wait to apply their

---

5   Stephen Covey, *The 7 Habits of Highly Effective People* (New York: Simon and Schuster, 2004).

solution to the challenge! They have every incentive to ensure it works. They're no longer dependent on you.

Quick tip here: the better you get at coaching, the more comfortable you'll get in posing questions and staying silent while your team member works out the answer. You have to be comfortable in that silence. The more comfortable you are, the better answers you'll get because that silence creates an environment where the team members can flourish. Your team may not be as comfortable with silence as you are and this will compel them to speak. That's how great answers emerge. As Susan Scott says in her book *Fierce Conversations,*

"LET SILENCE DO THE HEAVY LIFTING."[6]

COACHING IS A GOOD INVESTMENT

Some leaders might see coaching as just another expense, like the cost of an off-site retreat or something. But it's more of an investment in your business, like newer, faster computers or ergonomically beneficial office furniture, that improves your company's bottom line. That's because coaches change the game. It's like a professional basketball team. Sometimes you have five good players, but they don't win consistently until a new coach comes and installs a new system. Suddenly, your team is greater than the sum of its parts. Good players become great. Mediocre players start playing at a higher level. Everyone is operating differently and the results improve as a result. Coaching stimulates growth because you're challenging people and they respond with lasting improvements. They are not going to come back with the same problem over and over again because they solved it once before during your coaching session.

This also explains why professional and high-level college teams are loaded with trainers, coaches, and even therapists. It's because the teams

---

6   Susan Scott, *Fierce Conversations: Achieving Success at Work and in Life, One Conversation at a Time* (Viking, 2002), 218.

know that there will be a strong ROI on the expense of having these services. These experts ensure continuous improvement and observation feedback.

There's an expression: Don't feed the ducks. If you go to the pond every day and scatter stale bread for the ducks, the ducks come to know you, rely on you, and eventually become completely dependent on you. I had a client one time who was an outstanding salesperson. He was the best on his team, and at the end of the month, after he'd met his quota, he'd hand over leads to his teammates who hadn't made as many sales. He was feeding the ducks.

NO DUCKS ALLOWED!

"When you give sales away like that, people become dependent on you," I said. "When that happens, you're forever stuck feeding them sales; they never learn to do it on their own."

The same is true with coaching. If you're constantly reinforcing your value by answering team members' questions, you're not really a true leader. A true leader would sit down with the team members and guide them through the process of finding the answer themselves. That way, the problem doesn't repeat itself. You haven't fed the ducks so you don't have to worry about the ducks depending on you or suffering when you're not there to feed them.

As a leader, your team members might have different reasons for coming to you for answers. They might be new and unsure of themselves. They may lack confidence. They may have heard conflicting answers from others and need help sorting out the truth. Most likely, though, is that they have come to you because being told an answer is far easier than figuring it out alone.

For coaching to be transformative, leaders must assume that their imploring team member already *knows* the answer and is coming to you for confirmation. They're taking a shortcut and trying to get you to do something for them. We all have the ability to get the answers if we're motivated enough to find them. But most organizations have created an environment where the leaders are the problem-solvers. We want to get leaders away from the addiction of giving people the answers versus helping them find the answers themselves. And make no mistake: some leaders *are* addicted to being the authority. They feel important because everybody is coming to them for answers. You give them the answer, and they're grateful. It's a win-win, right?

Not exactly. All leaders with ready answers aren't really helping their team members grow, they're just making them less resourceful. It's like that old Chinese saying,

"YOU GIVE A MAN A FISH, YOU FEED HIM FOR A DAY. IF YOU TEACH A MAN TO FISH, YOU FEED HIM FOR A LIFETIME."

In other words, don't be so quick with your answers; teach your team member to catch their own fish.

I came face-to-face with a manager's addiction to giving answers when I worked in telecommunications. His name was Benedict, and he was directly managing one store and overseeing the work of several others as well. We noticed Benedict's store was underperforming and I asked him why.

"I spend about 75 percent of my day answering questions from all the managers under me," he replied. "I never have enough time to do my own work."

"Why are you giving them the answers?" I asked.

"Because they're asking me for them."

"Are you problem-solving with them or are you just giving them the answers?"

"I give them the answers. It's easier that way. I give them the answers, and I move on."

Well, if this isn't a coaching opportunity then I'll eat my hat, I thought. So I began a coaching program with Benedict. Over the next several weeks, I took him through the training and we developed practices that allowed him to use questions to help his managers find their own answers. Benedict was a great student, and before long his managers became far more independent and Benedict spent much less time with them on the phone. But losing that sense of importance and having all this extra time weighed on him. He felt he'd lost a lot of his value and he wasn't able to take that extra energy and turn his own store around. He actually *missed* that daily onslaught of calls. He missed being the guy who solved everyone else's problems. Eventually, he left the company and took a job with another company where he could again be the 911 dispatcher for a group of stores.

The point here is that coaching not only optimizes the people around you but gives you back your time and the freedom to grow your business. This might sound like a long-term investment, but it works and leads to sustainable growth and change in everyone.

HOW TRADITIONAL MANAGEMENT FAILS

The traditional way of management is for the leaders to decide their goals, develop a strategy to reach them, and then drop it down to the rest of the organization and say, "Do this. Do that." That creates problems. When we encounter companies that operate this way, they admit they have trouble getting teams to follow the strategy or carry out the job at a high level. There is a lot of inertia. There is more mediocrity than the company leaders expect. The reason for that is that the team members have no skin in the game. They didn't help set the goals or design the strategy. They weren't part of the process, so they have little stake in seeing it succeed. How many managers struggle to meet goals and blame their team members when in fact the true cause was the manager's lack of investment in their team?

It's a different story when organizations work in a circular formation with their teams. The leaders may have some ideas on where they want the organization to go, but the teams do the real work of establishing goals and strategies. When that happens, you typically see that 88 percent improvement in productivity we mentioned in the introduction. People support what they help create. They work harder when it's their idea that is on the line.

There is also a big improvement in the clarity of the mission when team members participate in goal- and strategy-setting. When you're co-creating and using the coaching process to create, everyone is part of the process and working to ensure everyone is aligned and on the same page. This is the big difference between telling and asking. Coaching is about engagement and ownership. Sometimes coaching is like a magic trick. You use questions to keep your audience engaged, much like the way a magician onstage has the entire audience's rapt attention.

It's also about candor and honesty. In a coaching culture, leaders hear what they *need* to hear rather than what they *want* to hear. The difference between a great coach and a good coach is that the great coach fosters an open atmosphere where team members can be frank. They can be honest with the leader about what they think is needed, regardless of how it might reflect on the leader. Of course, a forthright conversation requires that the leader understand that it's not their job to have all the answers or to insist that their answer is the correct one. Leaders have to be frank with themselves and understand that they are collaborating. They are not trying to get the team to a predetermined point but rather to a point where everyone has contributed and is enthused about the mission. Even if the leader's ideas are superior, what good are they if the team is indifferent about them and isn't motivated to execute them?

PRECONCEPTIONS ABOUT COACHING

A lot of people in business have misconceptions about coaching. They think coaches are for CEOs, or they confuse coaching with training or personalized improvement sessions for struggling employees. Some have had coaches in the past and didn't find it to be a rewarding experience. They felt they must have some flaws or performance issues that require special attention. The result is that they become guarded, defensive, and insecure. That's about the last thing you want. Coaching is not a performance review where you get corrected with a stick. It's also true that many coaches are merely pulling out information and distributing information and knowledge. Sometimes, they try to be more of a therapist or psychologist than a coach. They aren't getting the knowledge implemented or applied.

Our approach is different. In our system, coaches get that knowledge applied. They drive stronger accountability and execution. At every step, they are getting commitments and they are following up on those commitments. The result is that problems are being solved at every level—not just at the executive level. Our coaches are like John Wooden, the legendary basketball coach for UCLA. He had a standard for what he expected from his players and those standards were not negotiable. A big part of the coaching process is getting people to raise their standards and maintain that high standard because they know their coach is expecting it and looking for it.

The coach and coachee have a symbiotic relationship. Each one must show up 100 percent committed to the coaching session. You can't be a good coach unless you come fully invested. This means knowing how you left things with your coachee after the last session and what the coachee committed to do in the meantime. Remember, prior planning prevents poor performance.

The biggest problem with most coaching programs is not that people don't have answers. It's that they don't *act* on those answers. Leaders wait too long to have performance management conversations. Coaches are inconsistent in how they respond to certain situations, and they are inconsistent about following up and holding their coachees accountable. As a result, they frequently find themselves in a reactive rather than a proactive state. When a coaching system like ours is executed properly, there is a consistent conversation focused on moving things forward. Each conversation stems from the previous conversation and ends with a planned linkage to the next conversation. "Last time we met, we discussed ways your team might better manage closing calls because your numbers consistently fall below your goals. The idea that you put forward, which I loved, was to have a sub-team of your best closers focused solely on closing. Tell me, how is that going? Has that team been created? Has it improved your numbers?"

When a coach-leader holds his team members accountable for executing their plan, that frees the leader up to be proactive. They have time to look ahead because they're not bogged down daily dealing with an onslaught of questions or reacting to problems. A leader may think they're saving time by just answering the question, but in the long run, that approach is inefficient. You could have ten five-minute conversations about an issue or you could have one fifteen-minute conversation and never speak of it again. Extrapolate that over the hundreds of questions you get in a year and you have a boatload of time available to you.

Again, if you consider coaching an investment, this is your dividend. Your payout is that you get your time back.

ACCOUNTABILITY AND MOTIVATION

Many people hear the word "accountability" and immediately give it a negative connotation. If you're holding someone accountable, you're holding a club over their heads, ensuring they do their work. A lot of leaders behave that way, but I suspect the reason you're reading this book is because you don't want to be like that. I don't blame you.

The truth is that most people thrive in environments with accountability and discipline. That kind of culture provides structure, and consistency, and raises your team members' expectations. It goes back to the personal trainer analogy; if your team members go to the gym alone to achieve their personal fitness goals, there is less accountability than if they go to the gym with a personal trainer. When they have a personal trainer—that's you, by the way—there are more people helping them achieve their goals and pushing them. They're accountable to you. Because someone is pushing them to be their best, they start to see a different result. That result motivates them, even though the process of achieving it can, at times, be uncomfortable. There's a saying from author John C. Maxwell that applies:

> "MOTIVATION GETS YOU GOING, BUT
> DISCIPLINE KEEPS YOU GROWING."[7]

What Maxwell is talking about is someone putting structure (discipline) around what they actually want to do, and accountability is a key ingredient. Accountability is the difference between talking the talk and walking the walk. It's a matter of creating an environment where your team members must take action on what they have talked about doing. In this sense, accountability is not about being held to deadlines or getting punished for poor production. It's more about having someone who cares about their work and the quality of their work. Accountability

---

7   John C. Maxwell, *Fifteen Invaluable Laws of Growth: Live Them and Reach Your Potential* (Center Street, 2022), 69.

is not a negative thing. It's about collaborating and improving. For your team members, it's about hearing what they need to hear rather than what they want to hear. Do you want to be held accountable or do you want to be told you're performing well when the truth is that you aren't?

In the coming chapters, the process you'll learn will help you bring about this culture of accountability. The more you respect and practice these tools and the art of asking questions, the more effective they are and the better your results will be. Like any great method, it is both simple and deep. It's simple to start and execute but deep enough that you can endlessly work at your mastery of the tools. To get good at coaching, you have to put the time in. Remember what we say: "Good, better, or best. Never let it rest. Till your good is better and your better is best." I'm not sure who said that—it's been attributed to everyone from St. Jerome to basketball legend Tim Duncan—but it certainly applies to the practice of coaching.

Remember, too, that the recipe calls for a dash of faith. You have to trust the process. Radicle Growth starts with the plant pushing into the ground, out of sight. And, going back to an earlier analogy, the process is much like training your body through exercise. After a hard workout, you might be weak and sore. But in time, your body recovers and actually comes back stronger than before. People who embrace physical fitness must have faith that will happen.

If that metaphor doesn't work for you, here's another one: Every great question we ask is like a key that unlocks a door, including doors we didn't know existed. With every door we open we get closer to a solution. As long as you believe there are more doors, and you keep working to get through those doors, better answers will come. It's a continuous process of opening those doors until you find the right answers.

THROWING THE RIGHT PITCH

Building a strong coaching culture will help your company accelerate growth. The beauty of coaching with this method is that you are not painting everyone with the same brush. Each person is at a different stage of their career and comes in with different skill sets. The tools you'll learn with Radicle Growth allow you to grow each person individually. Mentoring helps leaders like you guide people from a technical perspective, but coaching encompasses human skills as well as technical skills.

As a former baseball pitcher, I sometimes compare coaching to my former pastime. As the coach (pitcher), you don't throw the same type of pitch to every player. Instead, you take into account whether they are batting right-handed or left-handed. Do they hit for power or placement? What type of pitches did they swing at the last time they were up? What kind of pitch are they expecting this time? As a pitcher, you might throw a few slow, tempting pitches just outside the strike zone to lull the batter before you throw a withering fastball that strikes them out.

When you ask a team member a sequence of questions, they might think you're looking for a specific answer, such as a certain amount of information. But really your questions are leading them to a bigger realization about themselves and the issue you're discussing with them.

Here's how a recent conversation between me and a CEO I was coaching went. We were discussing one of his team members' slipping performance.

"When did you see that this person was going off track?" I asked.

"Oh, it was a couple of months ago, I guess."

"Interesting," I said. "When did you make it your responsibility to talk to him rather than waiting until the situation worsened?"

"Just now," he replied. "I thought he'd figure out the problem on his own."

"Who would have benefited if you had intervened sooner?"

"Well, certainly he would have benefited. I would have benefited, too."

I wanted the CEO to realize that it was okay to be troubled by a team member's declining performance but also that he, the CEO, was partially responsible because he didn't say anything about it and instead made some assumptions. To put everything on the team member isn't fair because he had identified the team member was off track and still declined to hold the team member accountable.

"Would it be honest to say you share some blame?"

"That's fair," the CEO replied. "I should have acted sooner."

"Then let's focus on how we can correct this in the future."

SETTING STANDARDS—AND MAINTAINING THEM

I worked with another sales manager once whose team's performance was spotty and unpredictable. The manager himself was polished and disciplined, but his team was not. He maintained his own standards of performance but let his team basically do whatever they wanted.

One day, after having lunch together, we were walking back to his store and chatting about our kids. He mentioned that his daughter had just gotten her driver's license and was excited about the new freedom driving gave her. My son was nearing that age, too, so I asked him if he had set a curfew for his daughter.

"She has to be home by ten o'clock," he said.

"Okay, interesting. Why ten o'clock?" I asked.

"That seems like a safe time," he said. "She's got school the next day."

"Why is it important to you to have her home by ten?" I asked.

"Well, I want to know she's safe before I go to bed. And I like to catch up with her at the end of the day and see how she's doing."

"That sounds reasonable," I said. "What would you do if she started coming home at eleven o'clock?"

"Well, I'd take her keys away, and she wouldn't be able to go out at all," he said quickly. "She understands that, so we don't typically have a problem with missed curfews."

"I see. So you've set a standard and insist that she maintain that standard. What would happen if you didn't say anything to your daughter about missing curfew?"

"Well, she would just continue staying out late."

"Why?"

"Because I'm not saying anything."

"Hmm," I said. "I can't imagine that happening. You're too good of a dad to let things slide like that."

Suddenly, the sales manager stopped walking and turned to look at me.

"I am," he said.

"Yet, at your store…"

I didn't really need to finish my sentence because the message had already gotten through.

"I set a high standard for my family, but I don't have high standards for my team," he said and resumed walking with a thoughtful expression. At that moment, he realized what he needed to do at work. His perspective had changed.

The important part of the coaching process is that when you're able to change the way people see things, they are able to change the way they do things to achieve better results. Coaching is about changing a person's perspective. Many managers, particularly in sales, think that the priorities—of making sales and increasing revenue—outweigh shoddy behavior. They let things slide as long as everyone makes their quota. But the truth is that when you tighten operation standards and give your team better discipline, their performance improves, and their sales increase. You see this in professional sports a lot; the athletes who are sloppy in their private lives—they're getting into some kind of trouble or making poor choices—often then struggle on the field. You need to have balance on both sides of the fence. You need consistency, discipline, and standards.

The sales manager went back to his team. He knew he had to be vulnerable and transparent because he needed them to buy into this idea of higher standards and better discipline. So he had a difficult conversation with them. He took responsibility for letting things slide but promised that going forward he and the team needed to address the situation and make some changes. That was the only way they were going to achieve their goals. It took some time and a few more difficult conversations with individuals, but eventually, he instilled his own high standards and his team responded.

ASKING GOOD QUESTIONS

When using this technique, the key is to avoid asking questions that sound accusatory or put the team member on the defensive. Instead, simply be curious. When you ask questions out of curiosity, the question is easier to answer and the coachee gets comfortable answering. They become an open book, and you are able to transition to deeper and more detailed questions to uncover even more information. You create a sense with the coachee that you both are discovering something together. When you have that partnership, you can make massive transitions. Instead of the old-school mentality of saying, "This is what you're doing wrong, and you've got to do better," you are saying, "Let's work together to figure this out."

When you sound accusatory with your questions, you likely will trigger a defense mechanism that will cause your team members to clam up. This is not a constructive conversation, and it damages your relationship. You've put them on their heels when you would rather that they lean in and share enthusiastically what is happening and what they should do about it.

For example, coaches must be cautious when using a "why" question. Asking "Why?" can easily sound judgmental to the coachee and make them think you are probing for a mistake. This is more characteristic of the old coaching environment, where the coach tries to win the conversation. It's about right and wrong. In the Radicle Growth process, the coach isn't trying to win the conversation but rather get to a place where the coach and coachee can find a solution—the next step forward in solving a problem or improving performance. That approach creates a fun environment because you're working together toward a better future rather than being pushed in the direction a leader wants you to go. Again, the leader isn't solving the problem for the team members; they are guiding the team members to the solution so they come out of the conversation confident and eager to solve that problem.

This approach acknowledges that "everyone owns a piece of the truth," as Susan Scott puts it.[8] If there is, for example, an issue of poor perfor-

---

8   Scott, *Fierce Conversations*, 65.

mance with a team member, the leader has to take some responsibility for that. Perhaps the leader didn't train the team members properly or didn't follow up often enough. So, part of the conversation typically involves looking back and asking, "What should we have done differently, and when should we have done that?" When you do that, you often get the information you need to prevent that problem from recurring.

CHAPTER 1 GROWTH REFLECTION QUESTIONS AND ACTIVITIES

1. What kind of leader do you want to be and how do you want to influence those around you?
2. What is one area you want to improve in your relationships with the people you want to influence?
3. What are your personal standards as a leader and what would that list look like? How would you want to elevate them?
4. In what area of your job or life would great questions help support growth and engagement?

2

LEADERSHIP CHALLENGES

MANY MANAGERS WRONGLY BELIEVE THEY MUST KNOW ALL THE ANSWERS

"The leader's job is to lead and protect. Not to have all the answers, not to know everything to do, not to micromanage and tell people what to do or how to do it. A leader's job is to lead and protect. That's their job, and it's the people within the organization—their job is to get the work done."

—SIMON SINEK

Many of the people we train to be Radicle Growth coaches are new to leadership. Many have excelled as team members and have earned a promotion that calls for them to lead their former coworkers or to run new teams or divisions within their company.

These folks face a variety of challenges right off the bat. Although they may come to their new assignment with technical expertise, they frequently have received limited training on leadership techniques. Consequently, they tend to imitate their previous supervisors without much thought about whether that is the right technique or approach to use. It's also true that many enter their new role feeling either like they know everything about the team members and their jobs or that they *should* know everything. Perhaps they've always looked at bosses as people who are always right or know all the answers. As high performers, they want to emulate that. Some struggle to delegate work; these new leaders have built a reputation by *doing* and now they must move to the sideline and direct the players on the field. To preserve their status as leaders, they feel they have to know all the answers and many—as in the case of my former sales manager client—don't know how to coach others to perform better.

As a result, they develop a transactional style of leadership. They direct their team members on what to do and the best way to do it, and the team becomes dependent on them. Sometimes, when the plan doesn't work out, they don't take responsibility for the failure and blame you instead. That dynamic plays a big role in the finger-pointing you see in many leadership environments.

To avoid that, we coach you on how to develop partnerships with your team members. Through questions, the new leader coaxes team members to co-create a strategy that is being carried out by team members. If the plan falters, you have a relationship where no one gets blamed but team members are willing to assess what happened and make course corrections. In that way, the relationship between you and your team members is strengthened because the team knows you helped guide them to create the plan. In many ways, it's like teaching someone to ride a bike. You're there to get your team member started, but they are the ones who maintain their balance, push down on the pedals, and steer.

This process of guiding and being nonjudgmental calls for leaders to be firm and fair. You can't be fair and then firm. As the leader, you're there to provide structure and discipline. You're there to raise the team members' standards and create a consistent, predictable environment of follow-up and accountability. Your goal is not to forge a friendship but a respectful partnership.

Like you, the people you're coaching have some adjustments to make. They have to shift their understanding of what you expect from them. You're no longer asking them to carry out your directives to the letter. Instead, you ask them to take more responsibility for answers and execution. This can be frustrating for them at first. They come to you for answers, but you respond with questions of your own. They have to go through the self-reflection and the silences that can follow your questions and they have to become comfortable with your questions and in making their own determinations about what the answers are. In our experience, coaches who can gently push their team members out of their comfort zone develop stronger long-term relationships with those team members than traditional top-down managers.

You gain the team's respect by providing them with structure and a level of rigidity about following through. They don't feel they're being forced into taking more responsibility than they should. They feel you trust them to find answers and execute on them and this builds their confidence and motivation.

There is always a question about how personal you should get with your questions. Good coaches typically focus on three things: their job, their family, and their pastimes. There is a concept of "coaching the whole person," which means you have to get a sense of where this person is in their personal life and how that might affect their work. This knowledge might influence the pace at which you work with your coachee. If they are struggling in their private life and outside concerns are weighing them down emotionally, they may not be as responsive as other team members who have a clear head and are ready to be accountable and take on more responsibility.

THE NEUROSCIENCE OF QUESTIONS

Questions are a powerful tool. When you ask someone a question, it triggers a mental reflex known as "instinctive elaboration." The question takes over a person's thinking process and the brain cannot contemplate other matters. It's focused. Neuroscientists have shown time and again that humans are able to consider only one idea at a time, and the more challenging the question, the more single-minded people become about answering it.

Researchers have also learned that asking people about their future decisions creates something called the "mere measurement effect" that can influence that decision. For example in one 1993 study of more than 40,000 participants, asking someone if they would purchase a new car within six months increased their purchase rates by 35 percent.[9]

According to the World Institute for Action Learning, it all starts with trust. People must feel safe—and not fearful—to do their best work and advance their original ideas at work. Organizations with high trust levels outperform competitors by nearly 400 percent.[10] When coaches ask good questions, they form a connection with their coachee and send the message that they truly care about the team member's opinions and suggestions.

When you ask new leaders what they struggle with, most will tell you they find it hard to establish clarity with team members over the next steps. However, using questions and patiently having a back-and-forth conversation with a team member helps establish that clarity.

It is crucial, however, for coaches to have a clear purpose for each of those conversations. We'll talk about this more when we dive into the Radicle Growth technique, but it's important to note now that coaches need to prepare for conversations ahead of time. Later, we'll share some exercises that will help you with this and it will make more sense, but for now, understand that it saves time if coaches establish ahead of time what they hope to accomplish when they meet with a coachee. What are your objectives? Ask yourself, what is my opportunity to improve this person? You must build a performance plan to help them go from good to better and from better to best throughout the coaching process.

Every meeting should have a North Star—a central goal—and everything we build around this meeting should be supporting that North Star. You want to ensure everyone has clear expectations and clarity about what the path forward looks like.

---

9   David Hoffeld, "Want to Know What Your Brain Does When It Hears a Question?," Fast Company, February 21, 2017, https://www.fastcompany.com/3068341/want-to-know-what-your-brain-does-when-it-hears-a-question.

10   Ashley Reichheld and Amelia Dunlop, "4 Questions to Measure—and Boost—Customer Trust," Harvard Business Review, November 1, 2022, https://hbr.org/2022/11/4-questions-to-measure-and-boost-customer-trust?registration=success.

FOLLOWING THE MECHANICS

Another element of the coaching process is getting the team members focused on the mechanics of success. What actions will they need to take to succeed? Baseball provides a good analogy for this. If you're a pitcher, say, good throwing mechanics are crucial to your success. You have to understand the best windup, the best arm position, the proper release point, and an effective drive off the pitcher's mound. The coach and the player have to be on the same page when it comes to proper mechanics. Once you agree on the process, then it's about committing to the process and executing it. The coach is there to provide feedback on the mechanics. You're dropping your elbow. You're not getting enough power out of your legs when you drive forward. They also use questions. For example, as the pitching coach you might review film with the player of their pitching style and use questions to help the player focus. Where should you be driving off the mound? How is your arm angle? Where is your release point? Is it too high? Too low?

The goal during this part of the process is to get people to self-reflect, which drives self-awareness, and then self-actualization. Once they have that awareness, they can make changes to improve.

Consistency, discipline, and standards are crucial elements of this coaching journey. Let's use another example from the world of sports to explain this aspect.

Swimmer Michael Phelps is the most decorated Olympic athlete, winning twenty-eight medals. He qualified for his first Olympics when he was fifteen in 2000, won his first medal in 2004, and continued winning for the next twelve years until he retired in 2016. Phelps enjoyed consistent success and he did it through consistency in his preparation, consistency in training, consistency in recovery, and consistency in his mental preparation. Phelps, like other champions, had repeatable, programmable days, weeks, and months where his training and practices didn't vary because he had to be consistent if he wanted to remain the best swimmer in the world. Phelps often swam twice a day, seven days a week, and trained himself to be able to race at any hour of the day. This type of discipline prepared him to excel at foreign meets where adapting to odd meet times and time-zone changes was imperative. Boxer Floyd Mayweather used a similar strategy, often doing his training late at night because that's when most boxing matches are held. Finally, Phelps maintained the highest standard for himself. His standard was Olympic gold. He didn't go to the Olympics planning to win bronze or silver; he went to win gold. The reason Phelps is the winningest Olympic athlete of all time is not just because he was physically gifted, it was because he had consistent discipline and set standards that were probably higher than anyone he competed against.

Phelps is not the only prominent individual to demonstrate the value of consistency, discipline, and standards. Billionaire Elon Musk is another, and Steve Jobs was, too. In truth, there are very few highly successful people who don't have consistency, discipline, and standards programmed into their lives.

Many of them are continually raising their standard. As you move through the ranks, you improve technically or mechanically. However, as you progress, your competition keeps getting better, so you have to raise your personal standard if you want to stay on top. For example, you may start your career at a small mom-and-pop company and then progress into larger companies where your coworkers are better skilled, and the bosses expect more from their team members. When that happens, you have to raise your standards. If you're smart, you increase your standard before the environment does it for you. You can't be ahead of the game if you're always struggling to catch up. However, if you know the standard you want to achieve—for example, you decide you'd like to be a CEO someday—everything you do should be designed to bring you closer to that goal.

These are important lessons for new leaders to learn. In the old days, tough leaders and coaches were just the loudest people in the room. Today, the best leaders are those who are willing to ask more from people in a way that allows them to come across as caring and vulnerable. The biggest problem I see in organizations is that everyone's care level is off the charts but their candor levels are not. As a result, they fail to be direct with the person they're coaching. They always tell them what they *want* to hear rather than what they need to hear. The key is to find a balance between care and candor; only then will you be able to have transparent conversations that lead to transformative conversations.

A tough coach doesn't rule through intimidation. A great coach builds relationships and learns to be candid. They ask their team members to think bigger and to stretch what they believe is possible. The concept isn't just asking people to do more, however. The concept is getting them to believe they can do more and showing them that you believe they can do more as well. There is a unity between your belief system and their belief system. That's why when we work with companies and analyze how our training has helped them improve, they tell us they accomplish three times as much as before because the training increased their confidence. Team members developed a sense of empowerment; we believed in them and got them to think bigger. And when they thought bigger they raised their standard because someone was in their corner saying, "You got this."

It's not just setting higher standards and believing you can achieve them. Coaches also have to teach team members to take steps to achieve those higher standards.

HOLDING THEM TO A HIGHER STANDARD

This is why it's crucial that you hold your team members accountable. When their coach asks them about action items and deadlines, some people nod and make promises but don't follow through. Perhaps they've seen these initiatives before and expect them to fade away like others have in the past. But when you get to a second or third meeting and the coach notes that the coachee has not followed through on their commitment, the team members get the idea that this program is different. The coach wants to know what got in the way of them achieving their goals, and the team member realizes that their coach is committed. Their coach is going to keep asking about results.

In the old days, bosses expected their employees to arrive at meetings committed to improving. In this program, coaches are just as committed as the coachee. That's why they schedule follow-up meetings and keep track of the coachee's goals and action items. The coach knows what you promised because they wrote it down. That's why they follow up and ask the team member how to raise their standards. Not only was the coach listening, but the coach was fully connected to the process.

This process of being firm first and then fair establishes trust between the coach and team members. The coachees understand that they will be held to a certain standard but will have an opportunity to talk candidly about their progress toward meeting that standard. The coach collaborates with them, has faith in them, and has as much at stake in the process as the coachee.

Some team members respond immediately with great results. It's almost as if they have been waiting for this opportunity and jump at it when it arrives. They own it.

Others may be more resistant to the process. That doesn't mean they are bad employees but they may be jaded because they've seen initiatives like this in the past that have failed or simply faded away. For them, it's the new flavor of the month. But if the coach sticks to the process, digs in, and consistently follows up, it's just a matter of time before the team member responds favorably. It starts with the coach showing up and consistently being there with preparation, focus, and clarity about expectations. Some meetings may be less productive than the coach hoped, but they have to patiently stay with the process and keep the wheels spinning until they find some traction.

LEADING UP, DOWN, AND ACROSS

Radicle Growth coaches become true leaders. But they aren't always leading their team members or other direct reports. The skills coaches learn in this program also make them adept at leading across with their peers and leading up with their own supervisors. Stephen Covey once said that leadership is a choice, not a title.[11] When leading up, across,

---

11   Stephen R. Covey, *The 8th Habit: From Effectiveness to Greatness* (Free Press, 2004), 10.

and down through coaching, you make the choice to talk directly to people without using your title to be heard. When leading up, you make the choice to learn from your bosses. When leading down, you're nurturing future leaders. When leading across, you collaborate and support your peers in a way that you both benefit.

When I worked in telecommunications, I had a CEO one year who came to our firm after being president of Sony. At the time, we had over 250 stores, and the new CEO visited every one of them and met every employee. He did that to show his humility and confidence that he could learn from everybody in the organization, whether you'd been there twenty-five years or had just been hired the week before.

Regardless of who you are talking to, a Radicle Growth coach's goal is to never dominate a conversation. When you are strategically using questions, you should only be talking 10 percent to 20 percent of the time at most. Your big contribution is to mirror what your coachee is saying in a way that compels them to expand. You should be asking clarifying questions and follow-up questions. You're guiding the conversation, but you're doing it from a state of curiosity. You want people to feel heard.

We talked earlier about being prepared for a conversation and going into it with a clear objective. Another element of that preparation is visualizing how you want the conversation to go. Picture how the flow of questions and answers will go and create contingency plans based on what the coachee might say and how you will want to respond to that. In other words, simulate the conversation in your mind and practice what you might say beforehand. The best leaders in the world have already had those conversations twenty times before they get to the meeting. It goes back to the old saying, "Wars are won in the general senate, not on the battlefield."

SILENCE: LEAVE ROOM FOR THINKING

I recently worked with a team leader for a utility company that was managing a difficult digital transformation project. His name was Bob. He was having trouble getting his team to be accountable. They were not making progress on the transformation project, but when Bob tried to find out why, all he got from the team members was vague reassurances. Everything is fine, they said. Bob tried to inspire the team through education and encouragement, but the team members seemed reluctant to open up and speak frankly about the project.

Bob and I had talked about how to use questions, mirroring techniques, and silence to solve a puzzle, so we decided he would take this new approach with the team. He and I identified some questions he could ask. If the team hemmed and hawed and gave him more hazy replies, he'd mirror those replies in a curious, nonjudgmental way and then just leave silence. This would encourage the person to elaborate by giving them time to think independently, he hoped. He planned to use a stopwatch on his smartphone to measure how long it took a team member to respond, and he vowed not to be the person to break the silence. As Zig Ziglar says, "In a sales deal, the first person to break the silence loses the negotiation."

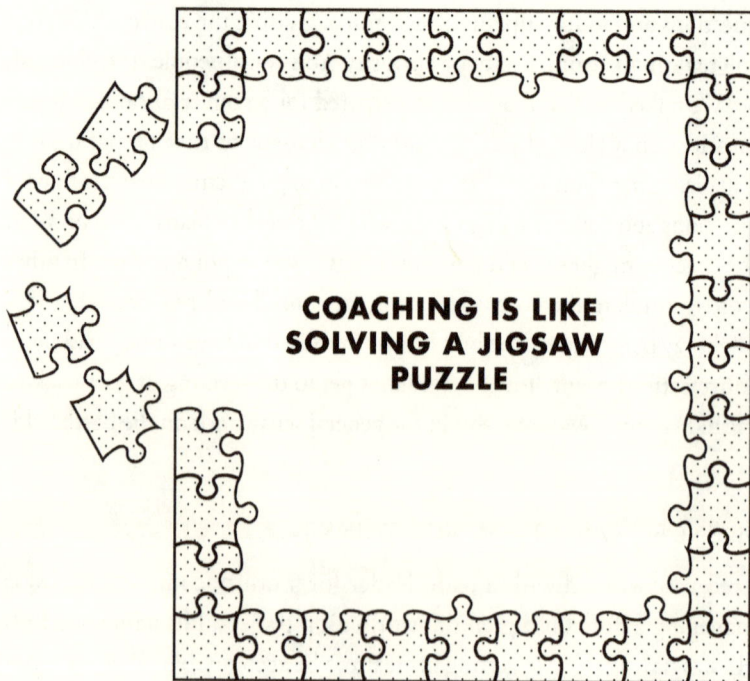

COACHING IS LIKE SOLVING A JIGSAW PUZZLE

Bob immediately noticed a big change.

"How's the project going?" he asked at the outset.

"Good! It's going fine," one team member said.

"It's going fine?" Bob asked. He held the phone in his lap beneath the table and started the stopwatch, sitting back as the question hung in the air.

"Yeah. Well, pretty much," the team member said after a few seconds.

"Pretty much?" Bob didn't seem alarmed or even particularly concerned, just curious.

More silence. This lasted seventeen seconds, but Bob later said it felt like four days.

"Well," one of the team members finally said, "we've had a few unexpected challenges with these people and certain elements that we feel are out of our control."

"You're feeling things are out of your control," Bob replied.

From there, Bob was able to patiently tease out more detail on what was causing the project to bog down. He was careful not to sound like a police interrogator or an investigative reporter looking for a smoking gun. He just leaned in and asked questions with authentic, caring interest.

"I NEVER SAID SO LITTLE AND ACCOMPLISHED SO MUCH IN A MEETING," HE TOLD ME LATER. "IT WAS AWKWARD AT FIRST, THE SILENCE, BUT I FOUGHT THE URGE TO FILL IN THE GAPS WITH TALK. BUT THAT SILENCE BROUGHT THE REALITY TO THE SURFACE, AND THAT ALLOWED ME TO FOLLOW UP WITH A QUESTION AND THEN WITH ANOTHER FOLLOW-UP QUESTION. SUDDENLY, THE MEETING TABLE SEEMED TO FILL UP WITH BITS OF INFORMATION THAT HADN'T SURFACED BEFORE."

Bob embraced his role as coach and began using questions to guide the work of not only this team but teams from other divisions. He shifted his strategy from trying to design projects himself to coaxing others, through coaching, to bring their ideas and execution to the table. It worked. In time, he was able to transform several managers into leaders through coaching.

CHAPTER 2 GROWTH REFLECTION QUESTIONS AND ACTIVITIES

1. Why are questions critical to building relationships?
2. Why does silence between each question enrich the depth of the responses?
3. Among those in your life or team, whose personal standards should be elevated?
4. Where would you like that standard to increase?
5. How would it impact their growth and performance?

3

WHAT DOES THE CURRENT CONVERSATION LOOK LIKE?

SOMETIMES THE TOUGH CONVERSATIONS ARE THE MOST PRODUCTIVE

"When we avoid difficult conversations, we trade short-term discomfort for long-term dysfunction."

—PETER BROMBERG

Dave was a salesman who worked in one of the cell phone stores I managed earlier in my career. When I first took the job, my boss indicated that Dave was underperforming and probably would have to be let go. My boss's opinion was based solely on Dave's sales results—not his personality or even his approach to the profession. So, his understanding of Dave and Dave's performance was strictly surface level.

When I sat down with Dave, I learned that he had previously worked as an appliance salesman and had done very well in that field. So I asked him about his sales approach on the appliance showroom floor. He happily went through his process and how he went about comparing different brands to each other and helping customers choose between the different varieties and features. One of his techniques was to scratch out a quick chart that compared how the different brands stacked up against their competition. He'd list price, warranty, and other features and this always helped him make sales.

"Great process," I said. "What do you think was the most important part of it?"

He fell silent and thought for a few minutes. "I guess I'd have to say the comparison chart," he said finally. "When I'd draw up the chart and show it to the customer, it was no longer a question of *if* they were going to buy a machine. It became a question of *which* machine they would buy."

I asked Dave a little more about his process. I was honestly curious. I'd been a cell phone salesperson myself, and I'd learned how to use pen and paper to help make a sale. In fact, we called the pen and paper our "sword and shield." But I'd never sketched out comparison charts the way Dave did. "Would the same process work for cell phones?" I asked.

Again, Dave fell silent for a time while he thought about it. You could hear the gears turning in his head. What criteria would he put in his chart? Which phones would be the best to compare? "I don't see why it *wouldn't* work for cell phones," he said finally.

"Why don't we try it and see what happens?" I said.

Dave and I made an appointment to check in again in two weeks. At our next meeting, we picked up where we left off. Had Dave started using a visual with customers? (He had.) Had it made a difference? (Yes.)

"I've used a visual with more than half of my customers," he said, "and my close rate is way higher when I use it."

It was like Dave had an epiphany. Through careful coaching, he'd found the answer to his difficulties. He hadn't been *told* what to do but had sorted it out for himself. He'd made the breakthrough on his own, and because of that, the experience was far more rewarding. This gave him the confidence to keep going and to find other solutions that helped him improve.

Over the next several meetings, Dave talked about his process and how he was honing it to be more effective. He now was using visuals with every customer and his sales numbers were skyrocketing. In fact, Dave soon was one of the highest-performing salespeople out of the hundred or so salespeople we had in our stores.

Not bad for a guy who was *this close* to being fired, right? Moreover, Dave's great success and newfound confidence allowed him to share his technique with other salespeople in the store, and by the end of the year, he was traveling to all our stores to train other salespeople in his process.

The coaching process is often about getting the coachee into a time machine where they go back and analyze what made them successful in the past and how they can apply that to the future. People sometimes shed the things that make them successful because they are trying to be more efficient. However, efficiency doesn't always drive long-term success; sometimes it just makes you do things quicker, and quicker isn't always better. Moving quicker didn't get them into the position they were in.

Dave's story also illustrates how important it is for coaches to be willing to have a tough conversation with a team member. As his coach, I considered it my job to get to know Dave, find out about his skills and processes, and work with him to uncover why his cell phone sales were so weak. A lot of supervisors just don't want to go there—either because they don't want to experience the emotional tension, don't trust themselves to say the right thing, or don't want to damage their relationships with their team members. They worry about how the other person will respond. As a result, pivotal conversations—such as the one I had with Dave about what he was doing wrong or what he could do better—never happened. However, if a coach is willing to dig deeper and find their employee's deeper truth through difficult conversations, the coach's questions will guide them to a discovery that increases ownership and execution.

Once you learn how to ask genuinely curious questions guided by your North Star, you can go into those conversations with greater confidence. You have a clear objective for the conversation, and you've jotted down what questions you might ask and how your coachee might respond to those questions. You have an overarching goal for the conversation and work hard during the talk to keep it focused on that key issue and not wander into other issues (which could be taken up in later coaching sessions).

SUPERFICIAL CONVERSATIONS

Bad conversations lack all those qualities. In an unhelpful conversation, the coach pokes around the symptoms rather than using questions to drill down to the root cause. True insights—such as Dave optimizing visuals to make sales—are gold nuggets that can only be found by digging. These nuggets rarely appear on the surface; you must work for them. In most cases, a person will give their coach a small strand of the truth and the coach has to tug gently on that strand and carefully pull the string out, inch by inch. Bad conversations stay at the surface. Your sales are low and you need to step it up. Bad conversations address outputs. They don't dig into the real root cause through questions, such as "Why are your sales down?" or "What are you modifying to improve sales?" You're not asking the team members to analyze, reflect, and assess.

Bad conversations are filled with what hostage negotiator Chris Voss called "counterfeit yeses" and false commitments. In a tough conversation about performance, a team member might vow to "turn this around." It sounds good until you realize that this person has never committed to anything and is merely trying to get out of the conversation. So, they give you a false commitment but fail to put action into it or feel the imperative to follow through. As a coach, it's a big mistake to let a conversation end on what might be a false commitment or a counterfeit yes. End it instead with a discussion about what the coachee will do before your next meeting to progress toward fulfilling the promise they've made.

A cornerstone of bad conversations is bad listening. In other words, people aren't listening when you speak, they are merely planning what they will say and waiting for you to finish so they can say it. There's a Native American proverb that says,

There is also a bit of sage advice from author Stephen Covey:

"SEEK FIRST TO UNDERSTAND, THEN TO BE UNDERSTOOD."[12]

A GOOD CONVERSATION

Most of the time when we hear someone is a great communicator, we understand that the person is an orator or something. They say profound things and convey complex ideas in a way that has real meaning and sticks with you. But the truth is that the best communicators are those who listen carefully and strive—through follow-up questions or repeating back to you what you just said—to fully understand your meaning. Listening is the most critical part of good communication. People talking with great communicators leave the conversation feeling like *they've been heard and understood*. There's no better feeling.

The effectiveness of any conversation also depends on focus and environment. You can't be distracted. You can't have a meaningful private conversation at an AC/DC concert, for example. Likewise, many people aren't set up to have conversations in the right context or right environment. You can't have an effective one-on-one conversation at a meeting that includes your entire team.

In contrast, a great conversation has a clear, stated purpose. The participants come prepared to listen and ask meaningful follow-up questions. They are not looking to win the conversation or come across as the smartest person or the best storyteller. Instead, they are looking for a mutually beneficial outcome. You have an objective that should be solved collectively because there are benefits for each party.

---

12   Stephen R. Covey, *The 7 Habits of Highly Effective People: Restoring the Character Ethic* (Simon and Schuster, 1989), 237.

For example, think about a coach setting up an appointment with a team member. The coach might say, "I'd love to get together and focus on how we can increase your sales," and they ask the coachee to bring recent data on KPIs and sales. That way, you're prepared to review a plan and proactively change it. The coachee bringing their own data to the meeting gives them—and not the coach—ownership of the record.

The type of questions you ask as a coach are crucial to an effective conversation. You want to start out with easy questions that get the coachee into a reflective state. They also have to get accustomed to their leader showing interest in their work, and easy, introductory-type questions help with that. If you're there to talk about weak sales and the coachee admits weak sales are a problem, you might ask what types of techniques they've used to change the direction of those sales. If they say sales are going great, you likely will need to pull out the data and ask about it before they'll admit they must improve. What do they consider great?

Open-ended questions followed by silence are the bread and butter of these conversations. You'll get a better outcome from an open-ended question than a confirmation yes-or-no question. Once they respond, you can use mirroring and continuation statements that help the conversation evolve.

It also helps to know the person you're talking to. There is no hard-and-fast rule about the questions you ask and the order in which you ask them. You need to be artful, at times, and understand that the personality or tendencies of the person opposite you will dictate the pace and tonality of your questions. The approach is always the same, but each scenario is custom-designed for the person. With some people, you may never have had a conversation like this and it feels right to formalize the process and prepare differently. With others, you can use a more informal or impromptu approach.

TRANSACTIONAL VERSUS TRANSFORMATIONAL CONVERSATIONS

Say you have two sales managers. Each wants to improve sales. The transactional manager will think of improving sales as a box they must check on their to-do list. It's an activity they have to accomplish. So they'll talk to the people they need to talk to and perhaps get some counterfeit yeses or flimsy commitments. But the action has no weight to it and whatever is accomplished is likely to fade quickly.

The transformational leader starts with probing questions and a deep interest in making improvements. The leader wants to have a lasting, transformational impact, so they commit to their team members and bring structure and accountability to the process. They rev up the engine because that's where transformative stuff happens. The two sales managers may have similar intentions, but the planning and mental preparation are far greater with the transformational leader than the transactional one. The transformational manager makes investments in their people day in and day out.

If you want transformational change, patience is not your best friend. You need to act quickly. It's not crucial that you push people but that you inspire them through really good conversations and sometimes tough conversations. As a leader, it's wise to determine if you are filling your team members' buckets or draining them. In each coaching conversation, ask yourself whether you are making an investment in the person or withdrawing from the emotional bank account you've created with that person. If you're just checking a box on your to-do list, your conversation with your coachee isn't making a big investment. But if you ask questions that elicit the team member's ownership of a process or an improvement, you are helping them fill their own bucket.

A crucial element of any conversation is identifying which obstacles are under the team member's control and which items aren't. Too many people put energy and time into things they can't control and this puts less of a light on areas they truly control and need to invest more in. If it's something under their control, you, as their coach, can ask how they react to overcome that obstacle. If it's out of their control, it's safe to ask why they are investing in something they can't do anything about.

CIRCLE OF CONTROL

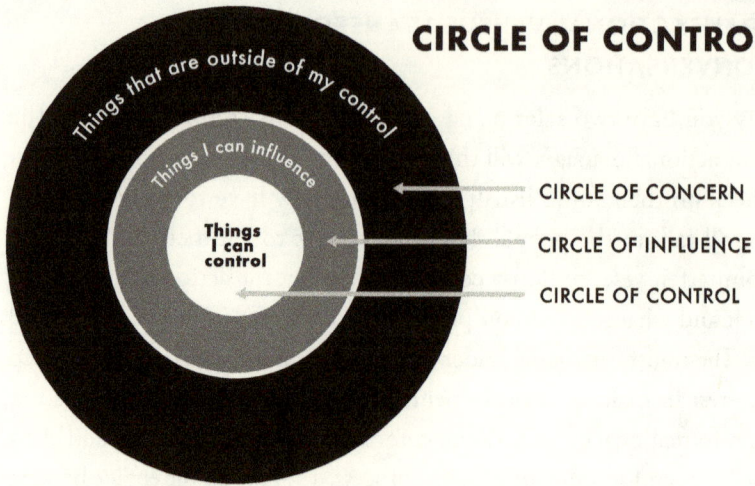

Things that are outside of my control

Things I can influence

Things I can control

CIRCLE OF CONCERN

CIRCLE OF INFLUENCE

CIRCLE OF CONTROL

In many workplaces, employees use noncontrollable things as excuses. For example, someone in retail might blame falling sales on reduced foot traffic to the mall. These excuses get accepted and the employee moves on. However, a popular saying attributed to motivational speaker Les Brown urges people to take action and pursue results rather than make excuses or find reasons for not achieving goals. Success comes from perseverance and proactive effort.

> "IF YOU SET GOALS AND GO AFTER THEM WITH ALL THE DETERMINATION YOU CAN MUSTER, YOUR GIFTS WILL TAKE YOU PLACES THAT WILL AMAZE YOU."

In other words, if it's not something they can control, then it shouldn't be considered a factor. Instead, they should be focused on the issues they can control. That's where they should make their investments. That's where their opportunities are. It's a waste to sacrifice your energy on issues you can't influence. Unfortunately, many leaders simply accept the excuse because that's easier than digging in and finding out why. They should ask, "When you ran into a challenge, how did you adapt?" or "After encountering that problem, did you reflect on what's possible to overcome it?"

In this sense, a great conversation eliminates excuses so you can concentrate on the things that truly matter. This keeps your team members honest. They identify you as someone who is not going to accept excuses. When someone becomes honest about the challenges they face, they start having fewer excuses, and you both can have meaningful conversations that bring transformation. As the leader, you must have the courage to stay there and identify what is in your team member's control and what isn't.

THE POWER OF CONVERSATION

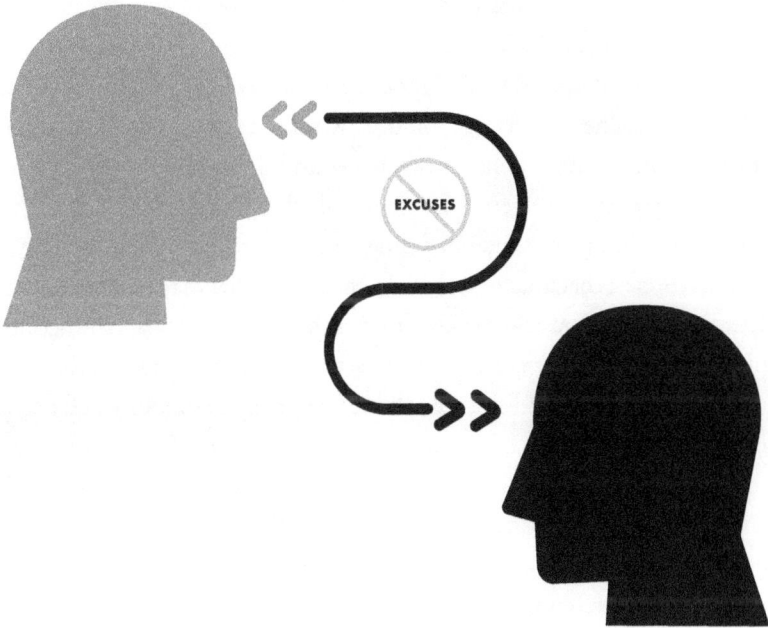

LINKING QUESTIONS

As we've mentioned before, each question you ask should emerge from the previous question and form the foundation for the next. It's a linear process that allows you to ask increasingly probing questions and unearth more golden nuggets. Your conversation is not only about keeping an eye on the objective but about keeping your questions linked. I frequently leverage "what else?" comments so the coachee keeps shoveling dirt and unearthing more nuggets.

"Hey, Matt! How are sales this month?"

"I'm having some real challenges this month."

"Really. What's your biggest challenge?"

"Follow-up with clients."

"Is there a certain type of client that poses the biggest follow-up challenge?"

What you're trying to do is isolate the problem. You are going from the leaves to the branches to the trunk to the roots.

As we'll learn in the next chapter about the Discovery phase of the Radicle Growth process, you might learn about several issues you want to talk to the coachee about. But you need to set the extras aside for another time to concentrate on one or two issues and dig into them. Too often when people have conversations they talk about sales, they talk about operations, they talk about scheduling, or structure. This is like treating a conversation or coaching session like a checklist rather than an investment. There is so much bouncing around that nothing gets settled and no action plan emerges to correct any of the issues affecting the team members.

There is no hard-and-fast rule about how many questions you'll need. But it's safe to say that if you ask only two questions before you start to solve the puzzle and give them feedback, then you haven't learned enough. Anyone who has watched *Wheel of Fortune* may have seen the occasional contestant who tries to solve a puzzle with only two letters on the board. It rarely works. You make assumptions because you haven't learned enough about their process and perspective. You don't know the battles they've gone through because you haven't dug deep enough yet. You may need to ask five or six questions that are connected before you spot that glimmer of a gold nugget and can say, "Tell me more about that."

Some people reading this might think the linear question approach is just another way of getting coachees to the answer the coach has known all along. The questions are just a way for the team members to take ownership. It's just top-down management in disguise.

What's different, however, is that this line of questioning helps coaches build a relationship with their team members. The more questions the coach asks, the more intense and revealing the conversation becomes. Sometimes, each question becomes a token or investment in that person. Questions asked out of authentic curiosity show care. You are making an investment in that person, building equity that you can draw on later. Team members reveal more than they ever have before and by the end of the conversation, there is a sense on both sides that they worked very hard to reach this conclusion. The coach asking all those questions has made them more vulnerable, and as Sigmund Freud said in some of his writing, such as his paper "Lines of Advance in Psychoanalytic Therapy,"

"OUT OF YOUR VULNERABILITIES WILL COME YOUR STRENGTHS."

CHAPTER 3 GROWTH REFLECTION QUESTIONS AND ACTIVITIES

1. Identify a tough conversation you are avoiding.
2. Who should you have that tough conversation with?
   A. Give one or two reasons why you are avoiding the conversation.
   B. What would be the ideal outcome—for you and the other person—of having that conversation?
3. How would navigating tough conversations impact your career and life?
4. How would consistent communication leading with questions improve your relationships?

4

DISCOVERY

EACH QUESTION AND ANSWER REVEALS A DETAIL OF THE BIG PICTURE

"The art and science of asking questions is the source of all knowledge."

—THOMAS BERGER

When a coach takes on a new client, it takes a while to unpack all the issues or opportunities the coachee is dealing with. In many ways, coaching is like solving a jigsaw puzzle.

The first step after you dump out all the pieces from the puzzle box is to turn over any piece that isn't showing yet. You have to reveal all the pieces before anything else can happen. Doing this, you get a sense of how the puzzle might work and which pieces might go into the middle, say, or in the upper right-hand corner.

THE DISCOVERY PROCESS

In the Discovery phase, it's important to ask many broad, basic questions. Each question and answer is like flipping over another piece to reveal the colors, patterns, and different shapes. You start to notice which pieces will form the straight outside edge of the puzzle. You notice that a certain type of red dominates the middle but a lighter shade seems to go from a lower section. So you start to roughly sort the pieces into the area of the puzzle you think they belong. And then you ask, "What do I want to do with the information I'm getting? Do I want to complete the outside border first or work on creating the central image?"

That's your strategy, and that's when you start building out your Discovery model that leads to self-awareness. The idea is to structure questions, collect data, and organize the data so you can lead into the next area around self-discovery.

Once you start getting answers about things like sales gaps, project delays, wobbly relationships, or poor communications, you must help your coachee sort through all that and decide which issues are the most important and must be solved first. Where should they start? What activity would bring the most value? Do you want to piece together the border first or work on that big central image?

MAKING DISCOVERIES

The Discovery stage, which typically takes place in one-on-one conversations between a coach and coachee, is designed to make team members feel comfortable answering the coach's questions.

IN DISCOVERY, THE KEY IS TO ASK BIG, BROAD QUESTIONS TO REVEAL AREAS THE COACHEE MIGHT WANT TO TALK ABOUT. FOR EXAMPLE, YOU MIGHT ASK, "HOW LONG HAVE YOU BEEN DOING THIS KIND OF WORK?" AND "WHAT'S THE BEST PART OF YOUR JOB?" OR "HOW DID YOU GET INTO THIS LINE OF WORK?" AS THE COACH, YOU'RE METHODICALLY TURNING OVER PUZZLE PIECES TO DISCOVER WHAT'S UNDERNEATH.

When some kind of detail emerges, you zoom in with more precise, probing questions. Say you're coaching a new member of your sales team. You want to discover what their goals or strengths are. So the conversation might go like this:

"What drew you to this line of work?"

"I got my first job doing this right out of college and realized I was pretty good at several aspects."

"Which aspects were you particularly good at?"

"Outreach. I was really good at outreach."

"That's great! What did you like about outreach?"

The Discovery stage is about finding out who the person is, how they operate, and what they excel at. It's not an interrogation. As their coach, you build their trust by being *authentically curious*, using their terms when mirroring their statements, and occasionally paraphrasing them and reflecting back on what they are telling you. This demonstrates that you are actively listening and shows how keen you are about clarity and understanding. In turn, they make your team members comfortable about opening up to you.

During the Discovery phase, coaches tend to use a lot of open-ended questions as opposed to close-ended yes-or-no questions. A good open-ended question might be, "How do our staff meetings compare to the staff meetings at your old firm?" or "What did you find most useful about our onboarding process?" or "What drew you to working for our company?" Open-ended questions are purposely broad and expansive and are designed to stimulate your coachee's thinking while fueling a longer, patient conversation whose primary purpose is to encourage sharing.

Discovery is not only for new managers or managers who get new team members. The Discovery phase can also be useful when you've been with a company for a long time and already know the players. Sarah, for instance, had worked for years with everyone at the table but still used open-ended questions to invite frank openness and—most importantly—uncover buried information.

Karen, another of our clients, had just taken over her division. She was familiar with the Radicle Growth process but wasn't sure if she would use Discovery in her new role. After all, she already knew everyone and was familiar with all the division processes. Her staff used to be her coworkers, her peers.

Still, she pretended that she was new to the company. In individual meetings with her team members, she admitted that she didn't want to make assumptions about how things worked. Instead, she wanted to hear from others how things worked. So, she asked many broad, open-ended questions and listened carefully to the answers. She quickly learned that some of the things she *assumed* were true were not, in fact, true at all. Moreover, she learned a lot about her former peers that she was unaware of. She learned about their professional aspirations. She learned about their private pressures. She even learned about their greatest joys and sorrows. Her team members also learned more about her, and their trust and respect increased during this reboot of Karen's Discovery phase.

Karen dodged a common mistake, which occurs when new leaders avoid asking questions because they are afraid the answer is obvious, or they assume they already know the answer. Many new leaders are sensitive about sounding naive or unqualified to do the job. During Discovery, it's actually a good idea to ask questions when you think the answer is obvious because you can learn if your assumptions are incorrect. Either you always had it wrong or things have changed. The answer you got a year or two ago can easily change, so consistent checks on key elements of the relationship are essential in coaching. You may need to rediscover the reality, and the best way to do that is by asking honest, open questions and listening intently to the responses. You can't rely on one person coming in with a stack of folders and saying: "Here's the current reality." Also, realities change and the answer you got a year ago or two weeks ago can change. Consistent checks on key elements of the relationship are essential in coaching. You must stroll the shoreline, turning over rocks and bending down to peer at what's been hiding in the damp earth. Think back to the former appliance salesman I talked about in Chapter 3. The company was ready to let him go. Instead, I had a long Discovery conversation and together we uncovered the absent link in his sales approach—the visuals—and he went on to great success.

TYPES OF QUESTIONS

In the accompanying graphic, I've created five categories of questions. For each category, I list the value of each type of question on the left-hand side of the chart and sample questions on the right-hand side.

The first category is open-ended questions, and it's followed by close-ended questions, probing questions, mirroring questions, and paraphrasing questions. While open-ended questions are a good way to jump-start a conversation, the other questions are what pry out the nutmeat. You may ask a simple open-ended question like, "How was the meeting?" But when the other person responds (as most people will) by saying, "Pretty good!" you likely will turn to probing questions to compel the person to share more. "What was the highlight?" you might ask or "What was the most significant decision?" Usually, the answers you get to these light probes lead to even more revelations, at which point you can start mirroring and paraphrasing to encourage the other person to be even more forthcoming.

QUESTION TYPES

OPEN-ENDED

Invite possibility
Broad and expansive
Open up options and ideas
Stimulate thought
Encourage continued conversation
Cannot be answered with a simple "yes" or "no"

"What items are critical to...?"
"How does this fit into the overall objective of...?"
"How does this differ from...?"
"What are the advantages and disadvantages of...?"
"What is on your mind today?"
"What else?"

CLOSED-ENDED

Narrow the focus
Help someone make a decision
Can invite clarity and specificity
Helpful when time is an issue
May end a conversation quickly

"Have you talked to...?"
"Will you be...?"
"Have you thought about...?"
"Are you ready to...?"
"Would you like to...?"

PROBING

Promotes digging deeper
Elicits more detail
Supports refinement and direction
Help to clarify a particular point
Aids in building a strategy to move forward

"Could you tell me more about...?"
"What if...?"
"How do you know...?"
"What impact do you think this may have if...?"
"What else?"

MIRROR

Nondirective
Encourages more detail without leading
Minimize misunderstandings

*Repeat back the last three or four words of
what the person just said as a question*

PARAPHRASE

Demonstrate active listening
Keeps communication open
Shows you strive for clarity and understanding
Thoughtful way to check up on inconsistent info

"May I play this back to you?"
"This is what I've heard so far..."
*"I would like to state this is my own words to
make sure that I understand this correctly."*

Remember that Discovery is about getting people used to hearing questions and opening up in their responses. You must ask questions with the quizzical interest of a third-grader and not with the unrelenting pressure of a grizzled police detective. That said, once the trust is built and the information flows, get in there and dig. "How was that decision more significant than the other decisions they made at the meeting?" "Was there much debate before the decision was made?" "What were the best opposing arguments?"

Discovery is primarily a fact-finding mission, and that's why broad, open-ended questions are so useful. You are collecting data. When we first start working with a company, we ask many Discovery questions. What is your process like? We might spend four or six weeks in Discovery because we want to know everything we can about the company and the people who work there. We're not trying to solve any problems. If you were starting work on a jigsaw puzzle, for example, Discovery is when you've dumped out all the pieces, turned over each piece, and arranged them by color or shape. This is all done in preparation to really focus on how those pieces fit together. The pieces represent the different topics we uncover in Discovery, and categorizing pieces is like prioritizing key topics you want to start with and build on to complete the puzzle.

I typically caution new leaders not to rush the Discovery process. Take your time. If you start giving advice after only two Discovery questions, you probably make some assumptions. You don't want that. You don't want to be the contestant on Wheel of Fortune who thinks they are ready to solve the puzzle when only two letters have been revealed. So take your time; you may ask five or six broad Discovery questions before you get some information that is worth drilling into. You may need to ask twenty or thirty questions before you unearth four or five gold nuggets that would be worth exploring in future conversations.

Journalists are professional fact finders, and journalism schools teach them that the key questions are who, what, where, when, why, and how. If you get answers, you can then write a story about who did what, where they did it, when the action occurred, and how the action was carried out. Finally, the story explores the why—why the event occurred and why readers should actually care about this event. In the coaching we teach, what and where questions are commonly used in Discovery and the others start to come in as you progress to Awareness, Focus, Commitment, and Follow-Up conversations, which we'll discuss in more detail in the coming chapters.

THE KEY QUESTIONS

Who? What? Where? When? Why? How?

"What" questions can take several forms. As a coach, you might ask your team member, "What do you want to discuss today?" or "What are your professional goals?" or "What do you see yourself doing in five years?" "What" questions help you establish the person's aspirations or desired outcomes, and they are an excellent way to establish rapport.

"Where" questions, meanwhile, help you assess the present situation, making them useful in Discovery. You might ask, "Where would you move to if you could?" or "Where in your current process do most problems arise?" or "Where are we in terms of our project timeline?" Some of these "where" questions start to heighten Awareness, which is fine—provided you have enough answers from your Discovery to focus on improving your coachee's awareness.

THE SEQUENCE OF QUESTIONS

While these early conversations are meant to be free-flowing, your questions should be designed to get increasingly revelatory. Although you might start a conversation with a question like "How are you doing today," subsequent questions should become increasingly purposeful. For example, here's a common sequence in the questioning process:

- How are you doing today?
- Do you have a goal that you are working toward?
- Will achieving this goal help you reach your target market?
- How will it help you reach your target?
- How is this goal different to you?
- How are you changing the way you approach the goal?
- If you hit this goal, how will it impact your long-term growth?
- Is this attainable in the time you've been given to work on it?
- Are you happy with the end result?
- Do you feel motivated by this achievement?

That last question about motivation might strike some as odd, but you are challenging the person to reveal what actually motivates them. Some people excel at hitting goals and objectives but those are not what truly motivates them. The question prompts them to open up and be vulnerable about saying whether those achievements are highly motivating or not. That is great information to have about someone. If this doesn't motivate them, what does? As a leader, it's crucial for you to know what drives your people so you can ensure they get those kinds of challenges. At some point, your boss is going to ask you to break down what motivates members of your team, and having had these conversations will prepare you to answer accurately.

Now, you wouldn't pose these questions in rapid-fire fashion. They are listed this way so you can see how questions become increasingly focused and personal. As your coachee opens up to the broader question and grows more comfortable in their conversation with you, you can use increasingly specific questions to gather more and more information and nuance. These tidbits are valuable as the relationship progresses to:

- Awareness, where you refine the "What" to "Why" to uncover the coachee's reality.
- Focus is when the two of you set goals and identify steps toward meeting a goal. This is the process of selecting what matters the most and why. You are narrowing the focus because focusing on less can help you achieve more—the "law of diminishing return."
- Commitment occurs when the coachee takes ownership of the process and makes action plans. Answering questions creates ownership in the person who answers them. They own the response. This is why "how" questions are so important; they encourage a commitment in the person responding.
- Follow-Up, which is when the coach holds their charge accountable, ensures there is recognition and reward, and connects the process to the outcome. If the outcome is not aligned with the goal or commitment, you may need reinforcement; reflect with the coachee to discover why and to eliminate excuses so you can reinforce the commitment.

All of these future steps will be discussed in more detail in the following chapters.

As I mentioned earlier, these conversations work well in private one-on-one settings. Although people can sometimes be more guarded in a public setting than they might be behind closed doors, we've had great success using this approach with groups and teams.

As you work through this process with your team members, it pays to periodically step back and assess what they're learning. The assessment boils down to five key questions that align with the five stages of Radicle Growth:

1. What did I learn from this? How many topics or categories came up? (Discovery stage)
2. How do I think about this today? What's changed about how I think about this? (Awareness)
3. Where can I apply what I learned? Which focus item is the most important to concentrate on? Do I have a narrowed focus because if I try to do too much, I might not accomplish anything—less is more? (Focus)
4. How am I going to achieve the goal? Do I have a clear plan on how I will achieve my objective? (Giving coachees ownership over the plan of action.) (Commitment)
5. Am I executing on what I say I am doing on a regular basis? Do I stick to my commitments? Is someone holding me accountable to my commitments (a.k.a., your accountability partner)? (Follow-Up)

Many companies are using these questions and formats as an auditing tool after staff meetings or planning sessions. What was our key takeaway from that meeting, and what are my responsibilities in relation to that? What should I focus on between now and our next meeting? Most people are already asking questions, but Radicle Growth is about getting them into an intentional influence model.

BUILDING TRUST

There are a variety of ways to build trust with your coachees. You should ask your questions out of authentic curiosity, and your follow-up questions should convey that you are truly interested in the other person's opinion and aren't trying to guide them to a preconceived idea that you, the leader, have already decided on. It also helps to show personal vulnerability before expecting others to open up. Being vulnerable isn't a parlor trick. It's impossible to fake vulnerability; you can try, but the person you're talking to will see that you aren't being authentic. True vulnerability is when you face uncertainty, risk, or some kind of emotional exposure. You are trying something new, leaving your comfort zone, and allowing the world to see (or hear about) the result.

Our culture typically views vulnerability as a weakness or an embarrassment. This is changing. People are starting to view vulnerability as daring to put yourself through something over which you have little control. That takes bravery and self-confidence. If you view it that way, it's more likely your coachees will, too, making it easier for the two of you to open up to each other. Feeling vulnerable is a natural part of life and our growth as individuals.

Remember, you're not a transactional coach. You're not putting your coachees through all the questions and vulnerability so you can check a box on a form to show your supervisor that you've been coaching. You are a transformational coach. You may have a process and a plan for your coaching, but you're not following the script on a form or checklist that you complete and turn in. Real coaching that starts with vulnerability may sound touchy-feely and soft, but people are willing to reveal more to those they care for than to some phony trying to complete KPIs for their annual review. As the adage goes,

> **"PEOPLE DON'T CARE HOW MUCH YOU KNOW**
> **UNTIL THEY KNOW HOW MUCH YOU CARE."**

If you fail to connect with people, they won't value your wisdom. They must know that you've got their back and believe in them.

To create transformative relationships, people need to believe the coach truly cares about them. If the coach is always dispensing advice and simply trying to create someone in their image, the process won't work, and the results won't last. It's not about being a guru. It's about guiding a person to a better understanding of themselves, with self-made ideas for improving themselves. People will be candid and courageous if they know you care about them. Some coaches think their job is to talk. It's not. Their job is to listen. Questions are the key.

QUESTIONS ARE THE KEY

Another way to gain trust is to ask the coachee's opinion on something you are struggling with. Ask for their help and defer to their greater experience and understanding of a certain area of topic. This reveals that you're humble and not so accomplished that you're not willing to seek help and guidance, even if it's from someone lower on the corporate ladder. It also elevates the coachee's confidence knowing that you've asked for their help. As Susan Scott notes in her book, *Fierce Conversations,*

"EVERYONE OWNS A PIECE OF THE TRUTH."[13]

---

13   Susan Scott, *Fierce Conversations: Achieving Success at Work and in Life, One Conversation at a Time* (Viking, 2002), 65.

What she means is that it's crucial that we acknowledge and value different perspectives because everyone brings a unique perspective that contributes to a more comprehensive understanding of the truth. You can also build trust by taking something they said and responding, "Hey, that's a great idea! How long have you been thinking about that?"

One mistake to avoid is cutting off Discovery before you gain deeper insights. If you rush to summarize and focus, you may be missing the best part of the journey. You may see the finish line before the coachee, but it's a mistake to take shortcuts to save time. If you jump in before the coachee sees the finish line you can do irreparable damage to the relationship. "Hmm," your coachee thinks. "Five minutes into a conversation and this guy's pretending like he knows what I'm good at and what I still need to work on."

The quickest way to lose trust is to try to solve the puzzle too quickly. It may take more time to continue asking easy Discovery questions, but it builds a stronger relationship between the two of you. Moreover, you're defeating a central purpose—to get the coachee to see the problem and the solution and commit to acting on them. When the coach jumps to a conclusion, it only deepens his team's dependence. They will feel no ownership in the decision and won't be motivated to help carry it out.

The best way to confirm that you've done Discovery correctly is by answering three main questions:

- What did I know going into the conversation?
- What did I want to learn from the conversation?
- What did I learn that changed my perspective?

Throughout the Radicle Growth process, it's crucial that you continually assess what you are learning and how you are applying what you learned.

CHAPTER 4 GROWTH REFLECTION QUESTIONS AND ACTIVITIES

1. Identify someone you want to go through the Discovery process with. They could be someone you already know or someone new.

2. Create ten Discovery questions for that person and then facilitate a Discovery session using those questions.

3. Write down what you have learned. Was what you heard what you expected to hear?

4. Create a list of areas you would like to know more about through a second Discovery session.

5. What is one thing you learned in the Discovery session that you didn't know before? How can you use that to support the next steps in the Discovery process?

5

AWARENESS

ONCE YOUR COACHEE DEVELOPS SELF-DIRECTED AWARENESS, THEY CAN TAKE THE STEPS TOWARD THE DESIRED RESULTS

"A workplace that encourages self-awareness is an environment where the most productive, curious, and innovative people thrive."

—NEIL BLUMENTHAL

Louis didn't realize he was doing a lousy job. As a content creator for a marketing agency, his job was to interview experts in the field and write articles based on their insights. While Louis conducted a lot of interviews, he did not write a lot of articles. The chief editor for the website contacted Louis's coach to discuss the problem.

"Louis is underperforming," the editor said. "He's not writing enough articles."

"Is he aware that he's underperforming?" his coach asked the editor.

"How could he not?" the editor replied.

The coach didn't want to assume anything so he agreed to talk to Louis. He started by asking some general Discovery questions to put

Louis at ease and eventually asked him, "How do you feel you're performing in your job?"

"I think I'm doing good," Louis replied.

"Okay," the coach replied. "What is good?"

"I mean that I'm getting faster and making fewer mistakes."

"Awesome! How would you describe your benchmark for success?"

Louis went on to explain how he felt it was his job to talk to as many thought leaders as possible so he could understand the professional landscape. It was only Wednesday, and he'd already conducted six interviews with influential CEOs.

"Is writing articles an important part of your job?"

"They're a part, sure," Louis said. "But the big thing is these interviews."

Quickly, the coach realized there was a gap between what Louis's bosses expected of him and what he thought they wanted. Louis was primarily being judged on the number of articles he wrote, but he thought the key measure of success was the calls he was making to thought leaders.

This is a classic example of the problems that occur when a coachee lacks self-awareness. As the conversation progressed, the coach was able to help Louis understand that his boat was pointed in the wrong direction. In time, Louis realized he needed to spend more time producing articles.

"How can we use *that* as a success metric between us?" the coach asked.

"I need to carve out more time for writing," Louis replied. "I'll do fewer calls but I'll spend time after each interview drafting articles."

In the Awareness stage of Radicle Growth coaching, coaches learn how to determine their coachees' level of self-awareness. Once the coachee develops a self-directed awareness, the coach can work with them to create the steps required to achieve the desired results.

A key piece of this process is helping a coachee clearly understand the "want-to" and "must-do" elements of their job. What are the things in your job that you love and would do for free? If the coachee can keep those elements in the mix, they will find their "must-dos" more enjoyable and certainly less onerous. In other words, when you prioritize their want-tos, they become more efficient with their must-dos. For example, when 3M created its "15 percent rule," the company encouraged employees to spend 15 percent of their time on a project or problem outside their regular job responsibilities that they were avidly drawn to—their want-tos. Several innovative products came directly from 3M's law, including Post-it notes, Scotchgard, Scotch-Brite, and Thinsulate insulation. Clearly, 3M was able to use their employees' want-tos to pollinate their have-tos and dramatically improve their business.

Awareness is the stage of the Radicle Growth process where the coachee owns the information they gleaned from Discovery and acknowledges the importance of it. It's the moment when the team member realizes their reality is not fully accurate and that they need to change their behavior to grow and improve. The biggest challenge is helping a coachee become aware of something they were not previously aware of. The secret is to focus on the desired outcome and work together to figure out a pathway forward. You must ensure it is *their* self-awareness, not yours.

THE SNO EXERCISE

The best way to create self-awareness is to guide the team members through what we call an SNO analysis. SNO stands for Strengths, Needs, and Opportunities and is our version of a SWOT (Strengths, Weaknesses, Opportunities, and Threats) analysis, which is common in business. This activity is a great way for the coachee to self-reflect and share, which helps equip the coach better for this and future sessions.

Here are the key elements for each stage of a SNO analysis.

STRENGTHS

The coachee examines their key abilities and what makes them stand out, including their:

- Professional qualifications
- Certifications
- Experience
- Successful projects
- Greatest successes
- Values
- Knowledge-based skills
- Human skills

Here are the key questions to ask:

- What do I do best?
- What separates me from everyone else?
- What do I do consistently that promotes growth?
- What strengths do I bring to my team?
- What experiences have helped build my effectiveness?

NEEDS

This is not intended to be a rundown of the coachee's weaknesses. It's more about leveraging questions like, "What would you need to be successful in this area?" So, you're not focusing on shortcomings but instead on what the coachee needs in terms of possible options for growth. The coachee should be identifying areas where they could expand their abilities through such things as:

- Additional training
- Additional resources
- Changing habits
- Avoiding certain areas
- Identifying areas that require more follow-through
- Communication mechanics
- Technical skills
- Establishing better discipline

Here are the key questions to ask:

- What systems do I need to be successful?
- What habits do I need to form to be more successful?
- How do I want to be supported and by whom?
- What resources would support my growth and development?
- What skills and/or training would be beneficial?
- Where are my performance and/or growth gaps?

Motivational speaker Tony Robbins discusses the importance of turning your "shoulds" into "musts."[14] He suggests that labeling a habit or practice a "must" makes our efforts to adopt that behavior more compelling and likely. When something becomes a "must," it becomes a nonnegotiable commitment rather than a vague goal.

"We don't get what we want; we get what we have to have," Robbins says.[15] "The difference between 'must' and 'should' is the life you want and the life you have."[16]

It's like the difference between the average person and an elite athlete. A lot of people talk about how they should work out, but an elite athlete talks about how they must work out to become the person they want to be. When you go to the gym, you expect to feel discomfort. You expect it to be hard. But when people think about growing their business or growing themselves, as soon as things become hard, they run away or stop doing it. But if you can realize that the discomfort is part of the process, you can embrace going through that comfort zone and into the growth zone.

---

14 Stefan James, "Tony Robbins: Top 10 Rules for Success and Fulfillment Revealed," *Project Life Mastery* (blog), accessed September 15, 2024, https://projectlifemastery.com/top-10-rules-for-success/.

15 Tony Robbins, "Tony Robbins: Turn Your 'Shoulds' into 'Musts,'" posted January 22, 2017, by Wealth in Wellness, YouTube, 2 mins., 15 sec. (00:48–00:54), https://www.youtube.com/watch?v=P-TiCROq9w4.

16 Tony Robbins, "If Your Goal Doesn't Scare You, Find a New Goal," *Tony Robbins* (blog), accessed September 15, 2024, https://www.tonyrobbins.com/blog/if-your-goal-doesnt-scare-you.

OPPORTUNITIES

We are surrounded by opportunities, but how do you identify the best opportunity for you? Opportunities are investments, so you need to be careful to make the right choice. You also need to be careful and not choose too many and lose focus. With that in mind, ask yourself, Are there opportunities in such things as:

- New advancements or changes in their industry?
- New technologies or trends they can use to their advantage?
- New positions they are interested in?
- New projects or efficiencies they are interested in working on?
- Opportunities for personal growth while keeping their goals in mind?

Here are the key questions to ask:

- What are my goals for the year?
- How can I implement identified support to improve performance?
- How can I use consistency and scheduling more effectively?
- What's the one thing I know I should be doing that, if I were doing it consistently, would bring massive growth?
- What's my most valuable opportunity?

Going through an SNO analysis with your team members forces them into a conversation where they must identify what they believe they are best at and why they feel that way. It also compels them to identify what their needs are and how filling those needs will help them improve. Finally, the opportunity section pushes them to create their own development plan. Again, this awareness must be self-directed. Only when the coachee freely declares what they need and who they are will they commit to reaching out for the opportunities.

An SNO analysis works on a micro level, where the coach and coachee assess the team member's actions in a discreet upcoming project, and on a macro level, such as when you evaluate an entire team and not just the individuals on the team. SNO analyses are good for coaches as well. What are the coach's strengths, needs, and opportunities? You can do a self-assessment or work with your coachees on that assessment.

CADENCE AND CONSISTENCY

A key piece of the Awareness element is incorporating inputs with connections to cadence and consistency. The inputs are the things that create the results—in Louis's case, for instance, inputs would be the articles he will start writing. The cadence refers to how frequently you create those inputs and consistency is about how steady your overall effort is.

A good example—and one that we'll return to from time to time in this book—might be someone who is trying to lose weight. Their inputs are that they plan to limit their caloric intake and exercise regularly. Their cadence is that they will eat no more than 1,600 calories a day and exercise three days a week. Their consistency would be measured over the coming weeks and months; how often are they maintaining their cadence of dietary restrictions and workouts? This is where the transition from Awareness to Commitment occurs.

One of the goals of the Awareness module is to expand the coachee's understanding of the goal-setting process, including measurement and accountability. From there, you and your coachee can create a scoreboard and learning path based on these goals. Here, the coachee is saying, "These are the behaviors I need to focus on to accomplish my goals. Here's how I'm going to track those behaviors and here's how often I'm going to be doing that behavior and tracking." This gives you a path to follow that's repeatable.

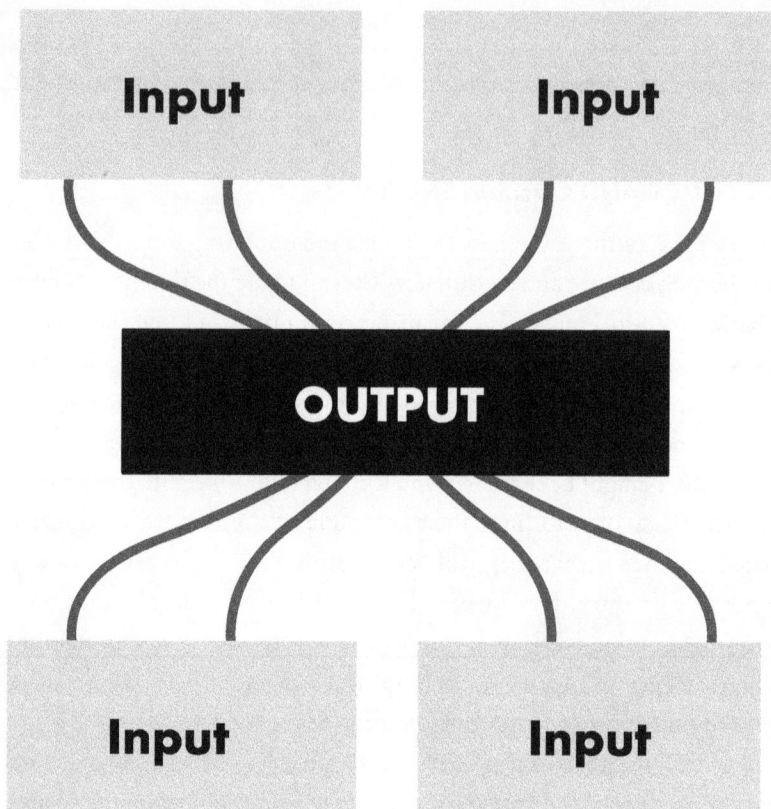

ACTIONS = RESULTS

The result of self-awareness is when the coach and coachee find the truth and agree on it together. The process is partnership-based. When you co-create and agree on what to do, when, and how often, the process becomes easier to move forward and succeed. Moreover, this process creates a permanent culture shift on your team; team members understand how you lead and what will be expected of them. This stage helps the coach get to the real conversation and past the "what do they want to hear" stage.

This process brings the coachee a sense of relief because they've been able to share and discover in a psychologically safe environment. They've gotten some truth on the table, and whether it's good or bad, they now have a path forward. They understand how to play the game better. That sense of relief, combined with newfound confidence, gives them an incredible boost. Their work is no longer shrouded in uncertainty or misconceptions. They understand the path forward and specifically what they must do to enjoy success.

Part of their relief comes from developing a relationship with a leader—their coach—that allows them to comfortably talk about their future. They may have been an average or even mediocre performer before, but with their coach's help and their own initiative, they understand how they can perform at an optimal level. They understand that they can be better but they also know their coach believes in them. A sense of calm enwraps their discussions as they work together to solve a problem. The coachee realizes that no one is threatening or attacking them.

Many people feel like they have to practically beat the truth out of people. But this approach allows the truth to emerge through calm, reasoned conversation. These are not high-pressure conversations that lead to a breakdown and a rebuilding process. It's a calming environment that challenges people to feel safe enough to be in silence while you both work to solve the puzzle. When you have epiphanies, you celebrate them together. That awareness provides a starting point on the map toward their goals.

They may have been living with the understanding that they are performing at eight or nine out of ten but learn they've actually been a six out of ten. That reality, while disappointing, can also be comforting because the fogginess and uncertainty have been cleared away and they know where they stand. It's better to know the performance gap and close it than to deny the gap altogether. It gives them a starting point to work their way up to an eight out of ten or better. Coming through this self-awareness stage brings order and inspiration to what had previously been disarray. They now have a clear understanding of where they are.

Keep in mind that it's best not to rush this process. Coaches should take their time with their questions and let the coachee arrive at their own understanding of reality. As a coach, it might be tempting to see the finish line and rush your coachee to it with an improvement plan. But a coach cannot force the realization on someone; the coachee must be delicately guided to the answers. Letting it come out naturally allows them to make better decisions.

WHAT IS SELF-AWARENESS?

Dr. Tasha Eurich, an organizational psychologist and author, wrote in the *Harvard Business Review* that people with self-awareness are more creative and confident.[17] They make better decisions, build more durable relationships, and communicate better. When we see ourselves more clearly, we're less likely to lie, cheat, or steal. Furthermore, self-aware people make better employees, get promoted more, and become the kind of leaders people want to work for. Their companies are more profitable than similar ones run by people with less self-awareness.

Although self-awareness is an attainable skill, and most people think they have it, Eurich's research revealed just how rare the attribute is. In her study of more than 5,000 people, fewer than 15 percent "fit the criteria" for self-awareness.[18]

Eurich says varying definitions of self-awareness have surfaced over the last fifty years, but her research concluded that there were two types: internal self-awareness, which measures our values, passions, behaviors, and personality characteristics, and external self-awareness, which measures how others see these qualities in us. People with internal self-awareness are less likely to be anxious or depressed and are more satisfied with their jobs and relationships. Those with external self-awareness—that is, those who understand how others see them—have better relationships with their employees and are generally considered to be effective leaders. There is no relationship between these two types of self-awareness; just because you have a strong sense of internal self-awareness doesn't mean

17   Tasha Eurich, "What Self-Awareness Really Is (and How to Cultivate It)," *Harvard Business Review*, January 4, 2018, https://hbr.org/2018/01/what-self-awareness-really-is-and-how-to-cultivate-it.

18   Eurich, "What Self-Awareness."

you have stronger external self-awareness. In fact, most of us have to actively work on both sides of the self-awareness coin. Just because you understand yourself, you still need to seek candid feedback from others.

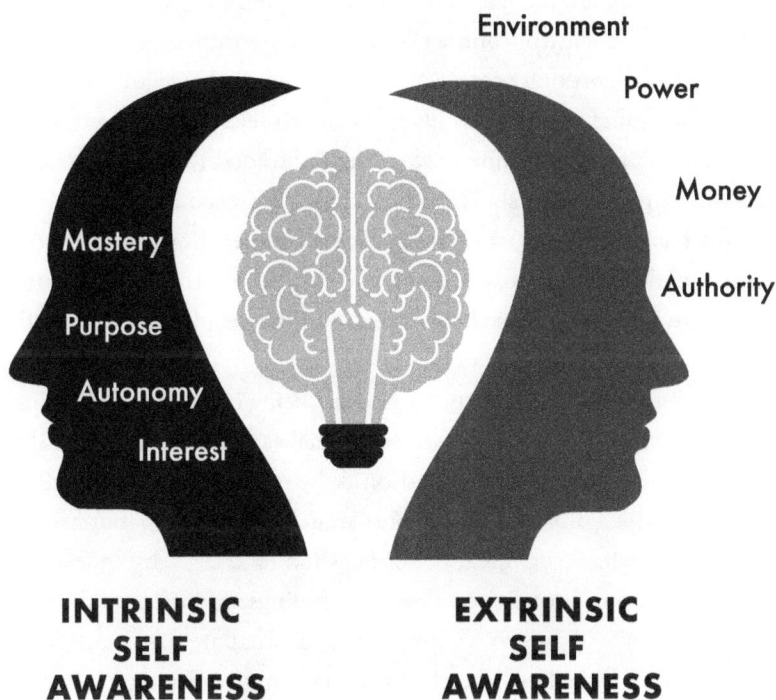

Environment

Power

Money

Authority

Mastery

Purpose

Autonomy

Interest

INTRINSIC SELF AWARENESS

EXTRINSIC SELF AWARENESS

"THE BOTTOM LINE IS THAT SELF-AWARENESS ISN'T ONE TRUTH," EURICH WROTE. "IT'S A DELICATE BALANCE OF TWO DISTINCT, EVEN COMPETING, VIEWPOINTS."[19]

19   Eurich, "What Self-Awareness."

DEVELOPING SELF-AWARENESS

Most of us have a lot to learn about self-awareness because some of it is counterintuitive. For example, experience doesn't do much to enhance self-awareness. We don't always learn from our mistakes, and the more experienced we are the less likely we are to question our assumptions, giving us a false sense of confidence about our performance. The higher we are on the corporate food chain, the more likely we are to overestimate our value and the less likely we are to seek and receive honest feedback. It's fairly common for experienced leaders to have a less accurate assessment of their skills as a boss than a less-experienced leader. It doesn't have to be that way. Great leaders, studies show, actively seek critical feedback from bosses, peers, and employees. They use the information to improve their self-awareness, and the people who work with them will notice the improvement.

Here's another counterintuitive finding: being introspective—asking, for instance, why we are the way we are—makes you less self-aware. The most common introspective question is "why"—why am I struggling with this project or why does my boss seem to dislike me—but Eurich argues that "what" is a much better question to ask. "Why" questions don't unlock our unconscious thoughts, feelings, and motives the way we think they will and so we invent answers that are often untrue. A good example is the boss who chews out a team member, regrets it, and concludes he isn't cut out for management. But the real reason was that he skipped lunch and had low blood sugar, which prompted him to uncharacteristically lash out.

So, skip the "why" questions and instead ask yourself "what." Rather than asking, "Why did I rip into Bob about those quarterly reports?" ask yourself, "What contributed to my unhelpful reaction to those quarterly reports?" With that question, you're free to consider any number of contributing factors, including the fact that you were "hangry" because you skipped lunch.

Leaders who coach team members need to consider the effect of "why" and "what" questions. When you steer your coachee to the "what" questions, you decrease what Eurich calls "unproductive rumination."

Bosses who lack self-awareness cause one set of problems but employees devoid of self-awareness cause another set altogether. They tend to communicate poorly and rarely admit their own mistakes. They don't listen very well and generally lack good emotional intelligence. They make excuses for their own missteps but are quick to criticize others. It's likely that the employee remains clueless because his former coaches avoided this difficult and emotional issue.

But you're not them. You are a Radicle Growth coach, and you do things differently. For starters, your style is not to take your coachee down a few notches with blunt statements about their emotional immaturity. Recriminations don't work well with people who are defensive and think they've done no wrong. Instead, your style is patiently asking questions that lead the employee to their own conclusions. Long before you get them interested in listening to feedback from others or analyzing what's repeatedly causing them problems, you establish a partnership with them. They come to trust you. They're beginning to understand that feedback is a positive thing, something they can use to their advantage. They're eager to work with you to become a better team member.

MEASURING SELF-AWARENESS

A question we often hear from coaches after an Awareness training session is, "How can I tell how self-aware someone is if I'm not particularly self-aware myself?"

Good question! If Eurich's statement that less than 15 percent of us are self-aware is true, how is a coach going to know if their coachee needs help in that area?

It's not as difficult as you might think. The truth is that many of us need to improve our self-awareness. We have to see our emotions and motivations in a clear-minded, objective way, and we have to be cognizant of our values, emotions, motivations, and behaviors in real time. We need to seek feedback from those we trust and respect. It's possible for us to be a "work in progress" while still helping others make progress on their own awareness. Remember, self-awareness is a skill we can learn and perfect, and what better way to build our own skill than to work with others on theirs?

Here are some characteristics of people who are self-aware or working their way to heightened self-awareness:

THEY LISTEN MORE THAN THEY SPEAK

As Stephen Covey once noted, "Most people do not listen with the intent to understand; they listen with the intent to reply."[20] Learning to listen closely and responding in a way that encourages your partner to reveal more is a key skill in the Radicle Growth process. It's also a vital skill for developing your own awareness. It's a practice you can model for your coachee.

"THE KEY TO GAINING MEANINGFUL SELF-AWARENESS THROUGH LISTENING IS TO MANAGE YOUR OWN THOUGHTS DURING A CONVERSATION," SAYS NICK WIGNALL, A CLINICAL PSYCHOLOGIST SPECIALIZING IN HELPING COMPANIES BUILD TRUST IN HIGH-PERFORMANCE TEAMS. "IT'S HARD TO TRULY LISTEN WHEN YOU'RE FORMULATING YOUR OWN

---

20   Stephen R. Covey, *The 7 Habits of Highly Effective People: Restoring the Character Ethic* (Simon and Schuster, 1989), 239.

IDEAS AND ONLY HALFWAY PAYING ATTENTION TO THEIRS. THIS MEANS BUILDING THE HABIT OF BEING A GOOD LISTENER IS MOSTLY ABOUT LEARNING TO UNDO UNHELPFUL HABITS. IF YOU CAN PRACTICE NOT LISTENING TO YOURSELF AND YOUR OWN IDEAS IN CONVERSATIONS, GENUINE, DEEP LISTENING WILL ARISE ON ITS OWN. AND MUCH-IMPROVED SELF-AWARENESS AS A RESULT."[21]

THEY'RE CURIOUS ABOUT THEIR OWN MIND

While being overly introspective can delay self-awareness and foster a self-critical inner voice, a self-aware person isn't afraid to question their thoughts in a curious, nonjudgmental way. Give yourself a break. Give yourself the benefit of the doubt. When your self-analysis starts to veer into the realm of unhelpful carping or emotional fault-finding, recognize and reframe it. Be gentle with yourself. Show some compassion, for crying out loud.

---

21   Nick Wignall, "5 Habits of Highly Self-Aware People," *Nick Wignall* (blog), February 17, 2020, https://nickwignall.com/self-aware-people/.

THEY SEEK OUT FEEDBACK AND ACT ON IT

Eurich advocates seeking input from "loving critics"—people you trust to be honest and fair with you. You can be this person for your coachee, or you can advise them to find someone else. The key is asking them how you can improve or overcome a difficulty—such as a recurring conflict at work. Does your advisor notice any patterns or tendencies that may be contributing to the problem? Fear of what they might hear holds many people back from this avenue to self-awareness, but Wingall offers a way to get past that.

> "THE MOST DIRECT WAY THROUGH THIS FEAR IS TO ASK YOURSELF STRAIGHT-UP: WOULD I RATHER HAVE A SMALL BUT FORCEFUL BLAST OF CRITICISM NOW OR YEARS AND DECADES OF NAGGING SELF-DOUBT AND UNDERHANDED CRITICISM THAT COMES FROM AVOIDING FACING MY SHORTCOMINGS?"[22]

As a leader, it's crucial to solicit criticism to demonstrate your willingness to lay your power down and lead by example. You have to show you can take it before you start dishing it out. You want to foster a culture of psychological safety, where employees are not afraid to speak up and share their opinions. Feedback is a gift. They know that the inevitable mistakes that happen on the job are responded to with support and understanding.

If you agree with the criticism, make visible changes based on the feedback. If the change is hard or will take some time, show them you're working toward it.

If you disagree with the criticism, try finding something they've said that you agree with and point it out. Offer your full, respectful explanation of why you disagree with their other statements.

True coaching is speaking to add value, not just to be heard. You're

---

22 Wignall, "5 Habits."

speaking about what matters most instead of what you think matters most to the people listening to you. When you're speaking for yourself and you're doing it in a vulnerable and transparent way, coaching becomes transformative. We internalize so much that when we vocalize some of these long-silent thoughts, there is a life-changing epiphany. Coaching is about trying to bring those things to the surface. Remember what inspirational author Seth Adam Smith is credited with saying: "When you speak your thoughts out, you give them light."

CHAPTER 5 GROWTH REFLECTION
QUESTIONS AND ACTIVITIES

1. Complete an SNO analysis for yourself and put two points in each category.
2. Thinking of internal self-awareness, write down three areas you believe others see in you that stand out most and why.
3. What is one way you could be more self-aware?

6

FOCUS AND COMMITMENT

SETTING GOALS AND A PLAN TO REACH THEM REQUIRES DRIVE AND INTENT

"Discipline is the bridge between goals and accomplishment."

—JIM ROHN

Through Discovery and Awareness, the coachee has brought themselves to the realization they have a few things to work on. While the temptation for some might be to throw up their hands and declare that this job "isn't for me," others are relieved to have developed a better awareness of what they need to do to succeed. The uncertainty about their performance is gone, and they now have a coach they feel is committed to helping them improve. The next step is to focus on specific goals and develop a detailed plan on how to reach them. The last thing you want from Discovery and Self-Awareness is a massive to-do list with twenty-five items. If you try to do them all, you fail to do any of them well.

How important are goals? They're crucial.

Studies of MBA candidates at prominent Ivy League schools revealed that 84 percent of the students had set no goals and 13 percent had goals but had not written them down nor had concrete plans for achieving them. Only 3 percent of the class had both written goals and concrete plans. After ten years, the students who had unwritten goals were making twice those with no goals, and the 3 percent who had written goals and a plan were making ten times as much as all of their classmates.[23] The study results were clear: to achieve your goals, you need to write them down and make a plan for achieving them. There is even a mnemonic device you can use called the five Ps: Prior Planning Prevents Poor Performance.

In the book *What They Don't Teach You at Harvard Business School: Notes from a Street-Smart Executive*, author Mark H. McCormack emphasizes that written goals are a crucial aspect of success in business and life. He encourages people to define their objectives and write them down to clarify their intentions, create focus, and increase the likelihood of achieving those goals.[24]

This is the stage we call Focus because setting goals and detailing a plan to reach them takes concentration and commitment. Coachees must cull through their goals and focus on just one or two of the most important ones. Then they and the coach need to be clear about what that goal specifically means, identify the first step toward reaching it, and then develop a scoreboard to measure their progress. This involves figuring out how to accomplish your "input" goal to achieve the "output" you want. For example, if your coachee has a goal of growing sales by 10 percent, they must be aware that they have to increase their call volume by 25 percent. Sales growth is the output goal and the increased number of sales calls is the input goal.

It is critical that coaches get their team members to narrow the focus of their input goal. While there may be ten or twenty different ways to achieve any goal, it's imperative to focus on just one or two that will have the biggest impact.

The coachee must be clear about what they are doing and have a

---

23 Maynard Brusman, "The Art of the Goal," Working Resources, accessed September 15, 2024, https://www.workingresources.com/professionaleffectivenessarticles/the-art-of-the-goal.html.

24 Mark H. McCormack, *What They Don't Teach You at Harvard Business School: Notes from a Street-Smart Executive* (Bantam Books, 1984), 213–214.

strong correlation or connection to the output goal. Again, a good example from the book *The 4 Disciplines of Execution* would be someone who wants to lose weight. Their goal is to lose thirty pounds by July 1 so they decide to focus on limiting calories to 1,500 a day and completing sixty-minute workouts three times a week. The person is clearly focused on the two factors that have the strongest correlation to weight loss. They know that "If I do this, I get this."[25]

To get that narrow focus, some coachees would benefit from compiling a list of, say, ten outputs and organizing them according to the highest degree of impact or importance. In the weight-loss example, the list might include drinking more water, cutting back on carbs, weighing yourself twice a day, and various other inputs. But as you go down that list to determine which ones are *the most important*, diet and exercise will lead the list.

The process is about isolating what action steps are necessary. Through Discovery and Awareness, the coachee has discovered a sense of reality. The question then becomes: Where do I strike? What's my action point? You can have all kinds of discovery and awareness and commitment but if you proceed without focus, you wind up doing too many things and not getting enough done.

Here's another way to look at it: the only difference between a light and a laser is focus. You want a concentrated effort on the thing that matters most. Write down your goals and the steps you'll take to reach them. You may find that the thing you thought was the most important didn't produce the results you wanted. There's nothing wrong with that, and when it happens, you move your focus to another input.

That said, it's important for the coachee to spend some time deciding on the right focus area. What data points support that as a top focus area? Also, what is the coachee passionate about in this focus area? Success rates skyrocket when the coachee has a passion and commitment to a specific focus area. The coachee has to have a connection that will enable them to execute that input on a daily basis.

---

25 Chris McChesney et al., *The 4 Disciplines of Execution: Achieving Your Wildly Important Goals* (Free Press, 2012), 12.

Before committing to a focus area, it's crucial that the coachee get multiple perspectives on what they are proposing to do. Other viewpoints can provide insight on why this is a good approach. Likewise, input from others may reveal that the approach has failed in the past. This kind of perspective can help you select your top one or two focus areas and you can go into the execution of those goals better prepared from learning what others' experience has been.

THE COACH'S ROLE

Although the coachee creates the goals and action steps, the coach is continually guiding the process. We are getting the coachee to bring issues to the surface and challenge them. Why are those actions important? If you're going to take action, where should you start? Instead of looking for confirmation, the coach is looking for commitments throughout the process. Discovery is about bringing all those things to the surface. Awareness is about bringing truth to them. Focus is about identifying the one or two things that will make the most difference, rather than the ten things that will flood you in a traditional setting. Commitment is about actually getting stuff done.

The Pareto Principle states that 20 percent of your behaviors produce 80 percent of your results.[26] This principle, named after economist Vilfredo Pareto, reminds us that the relationship between inputs and outputs is not always balanced. Some inputs have an outsized impact on your results. For example, I like to get up at 5:00 a.m. to prepare for my day—by working out, reviewing my schedule, and mentally preparing for what I hope to accomplish. That one-hour period amplifies everything I do over the next ten hours. The key is determining one thing or two things that return disproportionate results and ensuring you commit to those. When managing a team of 120 people, I asked what I did for them that had the greatest impact. Most cited our one-on-one meet-

---

26 Sarah Laoyan, "Understanding the Pareto Principle (the 80/20 Rule)," Asana, March 5, 2024, https://asana.com/resources/pareto-principle-80-20-rule.

ings. Those calls made them feel accountable and focused. So, instead of doing those meetings just once a month or once a quarter, I carved forty-five minutes out of each day to check with as many individuals as possible. That simple tactic translated into a massive impact on our team's overall results.

THE PARETO PRINCIPLE

20% Effort

80% Results

The point here is that we sometimes get stuck doing the 80 percent that produces only 20 percent and we give short shrift to the 20 percent that deliver 80 percent. Why is that? Sometimes we avoid the high-producing 20 percent because that work might seem more difficult or it might take us out of our comfort zone. Try to push through that perception; oftentimes, the 20 percent might not take any more time than the activities we perceive to be easier or within our comfort range. Think about those days when you come home and you say, "My gosh, I was so busy today." And then somebody says, "Well, what did you do?" And you can't remember what you did. That typically happens when you're doing the 80 percent that only gives you 20 percent. You're checking boxes and getting things done but you're not gaining much traction. Operationally, the 20 percent that gets you 80 percent are growth activities—the things that grow the business and make a difference. A lot of people think they need to do more to get more, but it's typically the opposite. We need to shift that paradigm.

We feel like we're not moving ourselves forward because we're not spending time in the right areas. So, the big question is this: Are you on the 80 percent side or the 20 percent side? Are you choosing wisely where you spend your time?

Frankly, most people don't choose wisely. When you focus on the 20 percent, that is usually proactive. You choose to go out and do that valuable endeavor. The 80 percent is the reactive work; it's the stuff you do when you're letting your day come after you and swallow you. The work acts on you rather than you acting on the work. To get to that 20 percent, you have to be purposeful and intentional. I worked with a million-dollar-a-year executive one time who frequently worked twelve-hour days, six or seven days a week. His 80 percent was daunting. Despite that, he spent an hour every day starting at nine o'clock and called as many as ten people—former clients, potential clients, even old friends—for the sole purpose of checking in and seeing how they were doing. He said that one activity delivered the greatest return on investment of anything he did.

The coaching process helps coachees distill their activities and find the 20 percent that matters most. Once they discover that thing, it becomes a question of how often they do that activity. Do they do it enough? Are you happy with the return you're getting on that behavior? If you did it more, would you get a higher return?

One thing our organization does well is getting people to execute. Most people delay and delay and live in a paralysis-by-analysis environment. However, if we can get people to commit to something that they thought of and want to execute, and you're in an environment where you have to follow up with that information in the next session, you're more likely to execute. You have accountability and ownership, and having one or two things instead of ten things allows you to put 100 percent into your top priorities rather than 20 percent into ten different things.

While the coachee is plotting their goals and action steps, it's crucial that the coach maintains an atmosphere of trust and support. A coach can't suddenly turn the process around and dictate the action plan; it has to come from the coachee because that's the only way to ensure the coachee is committed to success.

Again, the coach's job is to provide insight, not information. Use questions to guide the coachee through the process of identifying their focus and their action steps. Be an active listener and offer perspectives, not instructions.

What are some good questions to ask the coachee during this period? Here are a few:

- Why do we believe this is the right focus area?
- What data do we have that validates this as a top focus area?
- What are you passionate about? Do you have sufficient passion for these tasks to ensure you will carry them out?
- How will you ensure you are successful?
- How will you track progress?
- What goals have you set previously? What was effective? What wasn't?
- Who else on staff may have attempted these actions before? Have you talked with them about their experiences?

While all the stages of the Radicle Growth program are connected, Commitment and Follow-Up are perhaps more tightly bound than the others. That's because when the coachee makes a commitment, they know that the process involves a follow-up. The coach, the person who has committed their own time and effort to guide you through this process, is going to ask you if you did what you said you were going to do. They're going to know all the details of what you did and what the results were. So not only are you motivated by formulating your own plan, but you also feel an obligation to your coach to follow through.

Another motivational piece of this nexus of Commitment and Follow-Up is the idea of a consequence model. What is the consequence of not following through on your input goals? In other words, if you drop the ball on your commitment, what self-inflicted repercussions will result? This, again, is something the coachee must establish and that the coach must hold them accountable for. One guy I worked with took this element seriously; whenever he fell short of his input goals, he forced himself to contribute a significant amount of money to the campaign of a certain political figure he despised. This was a painful consequence, so he rarely failed to meet his commitment.

The point here is that if you have nothing to lose, your motivation tends to sag. Moreover, some people enjoy a motivational boost from the idea of losing or giving something up when you fail. It lights a fire under a lot of people. There has to be a consequence of losing, and it has to be something unpleasant to you. What is the coachee willing to put on the line to ensure they are motivated to meet their commitment?

THE COACHEE'S ROLE

Focus is about using a SMART perspective, too. SMART stands for Specific, Measurable, Attainable, Realistic, and Time-Based. Running your plan through the SMART filter can put some oomph to the effort. For example, you're not just saying you plan to work out three days a week. A focused strategy would be to work out three times a week by combining 20 percent cardio work with 80 percent strength work. You need detail when you're in focus. You can't be broad; you must be specific.

A key piece of this is developing a scoreboard. Here are the critical questions the scoreboard should answer:

1. What are the top two to three desired outcomes? Are these reasonable?
2. Why are these the top two to three desired outcomes?
3. Do these align with the company goals?
4. What are the benchmarks for these desired outcomes? Are these reasonable?
5. What are the necessary inputs for these desired outcomes? Are these the most effective?

6. How often are these inputs required and when are they required?
7. What's the relationship between the inputs you're providing on the scoreboard and the outputs you desire?
8. Who will be involved in this process? What support/resources will be needed?
9. How will progress be measured? Evaluated? How are you going to stay engaged with the scoreboard? What system will keep you focused and in front of the scoreboard?
10. What is the consequence model if the outcomes are not achieved?

MAKING THE COMMITMENT

Once your coachee has gone through Discovery, Awareness, and Focus, they have a broad sense of what they want to work on and have narrowed down their goals to just one or two items they want to hone in on. The coachee's search, understanding, and goals have all emerged from self-reflection and initiative, which helps make the coachee highly motivated to succeed. They own it. In many ways, Discovery and Awareness are the bow and arrow. Focus is about identifying the target.

Unfortunately, many team members reach this stage, and all progress stops. They lose their resolve because no one has gotten them to commit to specific steps on a timeline.

Radicle Growth solves this problem at the Commitment stage, which is when the coach uses guiding questions to help their team member build their action steps into their schedule. The coachee's ownership is strong because their commitment wasn't given to them but instead was created by them. Here's how that line of questioning might go:

- Why are these action steps you've identified the most important?
- How are you going to incorporate them into your schedule?
- Why do you believe these steps will create the change you want to see?
- How will you measure your progress?

- What are the self-imposed consequences if you fail to keep your commitment?
- When are you going to start?

In short, the coach's goal is to get the coachee to say what they are going to do, when they are going to do it, why they are going to do it, and how they are going to measure the results. As negotiation expert Chris Voss says in his book *Never Split the Difference,*

"'YES' IS NOTHING WITHOUT 'HOW.'"[27]

The coachee gives their personal commitment to take action on those items they have discovered on their own through this guided process. The coach isn't issuing directives and deadlines the way they might in a traditional environment. Instead, they let the coachee set the cadence and commitment and the coach holds the coachee accountable to take the steps the coachee has identified themselves.

To use the weight-loss analogy again, the coach says, "You've decided that losing twenty pounds by July 1 will require that you cut down on calories and increase your exercise. Fantastic! All the data suggests this is the most reliable approach to losing weight."

"Yes, I think it's clear this is the best approach."

"So tell me, exactly how much less will you eat?"

"Well, I think I'll look to reduce my caloric intake by 20 percent."

"Awesome. What does that look like?"

"Oh. Yeah. Well, I guess I'll cut out those late-night snacks I love. And no more french fries!"

"How are you planning to measure your caloric intake? How often will you measure it?"

---

27 Chris Voss and Tahl Raz, *Never Split the Difference: Negotiating as If Your Life Depended on It* (Harper Business, 2016), 163, 164.

"I found an online calculator that I plan to use. I'll measure my meals every day and record it in my journal. This will help keep me honest."

"Excellent! Would you mind bringing your journal with you to the next session? I'd love to see how you do this. Maybe I can imitate you and lose this jelly roll I've got!"

"You bet. My system might help you!"

"I hope so. Now, tell me: How often are you going to work out?"

"My goal is to exercise every day, even on Sunday. I'll swim on Monday, Wednesday, and Friday and jog or ride my bike on the other days."

"How will you track those results?"

"On my watch! I have an Apple watch that measures heart rate, calories burned, and distance traveled. It even counts my laps when I'm swimming. It saves all this data on an app I've installed on my phone, so I'll be able to get daily and weekly reports on whether I've achieved preset exercise goals."

"Well, it sounds like you've got this figured out! Would you mind keeping me posted on your progress?"

"Absolutely!"

This same kind of clarity and commitment between coach and coachee works just as well when talking about work. Perhaps the coachee has committed to improving sales and plans to increase his number of calls and shorten the time between an initial call and a follow-up. The coachee's actions and results can all be documented and shared regularly with their coach.

The goal for the coach is to be in full alignment with the coachee on what measurable behaviors they plan to do with commitments on time and delivery. Both sides understand exactly what will be done and when it will be done. There is also an understanding that the coach will ask them to recount their efforts in their next meeting. The coachee leaves the meeting highly committed: they developed a plan for themselves and they know that their coach will be asking for progress reports and documented results. Those two factors make it highly unlikely that the coachee will disregard the promises and commitments they've made.

"So, when we meet next week, you should have records of what you ate and how many calories you consumed over those seven days. Bring your workout log that also shows what exercises you did and how long you spent working out. What other data would be useful for us to have?" The coach uses the coachee's goals and action steps as commitment points the coach will go through with them. In that situation, the coachee is validating the detail, commitment, and connection they have made. They own everything because it all originally came from them. The commitment and ownership come from them. The coach is the voice on the other side of the table that holds them accountable.

Commitment and the next stage (Follow-Up) are where you make the process truly accountable because then people need to show up. They either did it or didn't do it. The coach needs to understand that process. If the coachee came through and fulfilled their commitment, let's review the results. If the coachee failed to complete the commitment, let's talk about what stood in the way and how we will get around it in the future. Coaches must understand that habits are difficult to form—not because behaviors are difficult but because consistency is difficult.

CONSISTENCY, DISCIPLINE, AND STANDARDS

These three concepts—consistency, discipline, and standards—play a big role in the commitment stage.

Consider two athletes who have equal abilities and conditioning. Each is training under an identical program—same regimen, same coaches, same training duration. What separates them is their level of intensity, consistency, discipline, and standards. The better athlete will work out with more concentration. They never miss a practice, and they always execute techniques with precision and focus. They are continually raising their standards as their skills and fitness improve. They never lower their standard or negotiate it.

The best athlete is also completely aligned with their coach. Their goals are written down and their progress toward them is measured and recorded as well. There should be no doubt or misunderstanding between the coach and coachee over what the coachee's goals are. Both sides should know exactly what will happen and when.

Intensity is another factor. Here's an example. We were working with one team that wanted to expand its business and had decided the input goal was an extra forty-five calls a week. When we followed up with them, the team members said they had reached that input goal and that each had carefully followed the script. But when we listened to the calls, the tonality was barely measured on the intensity meter. The calls lacked urgency or energy of any sort. The callers read the script with a kind of toneless lethargy. Nobody was going to buy anything from callers like that. The moral of the story is that you can follow standards all you want—such as reading the pitch script word for word—but if your effort lacks intensity, you won't succeed. You're no better off than the person who goes to the gym and sits on an exercise bike for an hour without pedaling. Intensity makes all the difference.

Consistency is equally important. In fact, when you start taking action steps, it's probably more important to be committed to the process than to have immediate success.

As James Clear notes in his book *Atomic Habits*, "You do not rise to the level of your goals. You fall to the level of your systems."[28]

Studies examining groups trying to lose weight have found that those recognized for being committed to the weight-loss process lost significantly more weight than those who were recognized for their weight-loss results. If your mindset is on the number and not on a commitment to the process, it's likely that you'll give up easily. However, if you focus on the commitment to the process, you're more likely to stick to it, and eventually, the results will speak for themselves.

What often happens is people get going, and they get momentum and their bosses start recognizing them for producing an outcome. That's fine; it's nice to recognize when someone achieves something. But focusing too much on the outcome is counter to long-term growth and consistency. However, if you start recognizing their commitment

---

28 James Clear, *Atomic Habits: An Easy and Proven Way to Build Good Habits and Break Bad Ones* (Avery, 2018), 27.

to getting up at 5:00 a.m., their commitment to going to the gym, and their commitment to running every day, it's less about the outcome and more about feeding the process. When you feed the process, and people lean into it, they become more consistent, and the best results always come from consistent processes. The results don't continue unless you have a good process, and consistency is the catalyst. When you recognize consistent discipline, you see world-class results.

There's an adage for that as well: respect the process and recognize the results. In our training, we like to incorporate author Mark Sanborn's ideas about getting the maximum benefit from practice by using what he calls the F.I.T. technique. F.I.T. stands for frequency, intensity, and technique; doing all or any of those things translates into performance improvement.[29]

THE F.I.T. TECHNIQUE

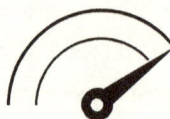

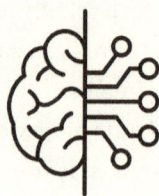

Frequency   Intensity   Technique

---

29 Mark Sanborn, "Think You've Reached the Top? There's Always a Way to Improve: The Goal of the Best Is to Keep Getting Better," *Entrepreneur*, September 15, 2017, https://www.entrepreneur.com/living/think-youve-reached-the-top-theres-always-a-way-to/300360.

Having a timeline is equally critical. The best example of that is when President John F. Kennedy declared in the early sixties that the United States would put a man on the moon within a decade. Did that increase accountability at NASA or decrease it? Obviously, it increased it. NASA made a massive commitment and stuck to the timeline. If your commitment to a timeline is loose, then you really don't have a timeline at all. Wiggle room is the enemy of any timeline or commitment. You have to be clear about your timeline and follow it.

Most people are not used to a culture of timelines, commitments, and accountability. Some individuals might argue that they have hard-and-fast timelines, but if you look closely, you see that they don't have people following up with them who are as committed to that timeline as they are. Our process is about a commitment between two parties on commitments and timelines. That's where the intensity comes from. This is not just *your* goal, this is *our* goal.

In a culture of accountability, you create a relationship between the coach and the coachee around getting certain things done. You know exactly what the commitments are. You know exactly what the follow-through needs to be. Admittedly, some bosses complain that they have trouble getting their team members to commit to a goal or commit to the process. When I hear that, I always ask, "Well, are you telling them or asking them to do something?" It's usually a variety of scenarios that cause this, but in most cases, there is no ownership on the part of the coachee. It's not their idea, and they lack incentive to follow through. But when it's their idea and not the boss's, there is a whole new dynamic involved: ownership. Our process is focused on getting ownership over a particular action plan; when you do that, it cements the commitment.

As famed negotiator Chris Voss says,

"'YES' IS NOTHING WITHOUT 'HOW.'"[30]

30   Voss and Raz, *Never Split*, 163, 164.

In other words, people can sound committed but aren't actually committed. They like to talk the talk, but they don't walk the walk. Something is holding them back. Perhaps failure is holding them back. But in this system and in this culture, it doesn't matter if you walk and then fall, as long as you get back up and start walking again. I would rather have someone who is doing all kinds of action and failing than someone who talks a good game but does nothing. My message to them is: Go fail. At least make an effort at it and commit to the process. The people who are successful long-term are those who commit to testing it, trying it, and taking action on it.

CHAPTER 6 GROWTH REFLECTION QUESTIONS AND ACTIVITIES

1. After reading about the Pareto Principle, which asserts that 20 percent of your behavior will produce 80 percent of your results, what are two behaviors you do on a regular basis that produce your highest return on investment?

2. Use the following questions to develop your "focus" goal:
   A. Why are these action steps you've identified the most important?
   B. How are you going to incorporate them into your schedule?
   C. Why do you believe these steps will create the change you want to see?
   D. How will you measure your progress?
   E. What are the self-imposed consequences if you fail to keep your commitment?
   F. When are you going to start?

7

FOLLOW-UP

DON'T MISS THE OPPORTUNITY TO CELEBRATE SUCCESS

"Good ideas are not adopted automatically. They must be driven into practice with courageous impatience. Once implemented they can be easily over-turned or subverted through apathy or lack of follow-up, so a continuous effort is required."

—HYMAN RICKOVER

This is not your victory lap. This is not the time when you, as a coach, get to relax and congratulate your coachee and yourself for a job well done.

The Follow-Up stage of the Radicle Growth coaching program is instead a crucial moment that, if taken seriously, propels you and your coachee into a successful pattern of continuous improvement and success. If follow-up is not taken seriously, all your work up to now can easily collapse. The follow-up is where the coach confirms that what the coachee proposed doing was actually completed successfully. Done right, follow-up solidifies and builds on the trust you and your coachee have established. If the follow-up is executed poorly, that trust can evaporate.

Unfortunately, the follow-up is where a lot of coaches fall down.

They have spent so much time and effort working with the coachee on discovery, awareness, focus, and commitment that they ease back and refocus on their other responsibilities, thinking that the bulk of their work so far with their team members is sufficient. They think the momentum they've created is ample enough to carry their coachee on to success. As a result, their follow-up sessions are delayed or lack the same urgency as their previous sessions. They don't bother to confirm that the coachee accomplished what they set out to do. This is a huge mistake.

The follow-up is actually a pivotal moment. The coachee has been working hard to execute their own ideas, and the follow-up is the coach's opportunity to affirm that all that work was valuable. What did you achieve? How did you do it? What did you learn in the process? Show me your numbers! The coach must go into this conversation with the same level of preparation and enthusiasm as they have in all the previous sessions with their coachee.

WHEN THE COACH DOESN'T SHOW UP

The coach can actually do a great deal of damage if they allow their commitment to lapse at the Follow-Up stage. The coach and the coachee need to be equally contributing to the relationship. In the old days of coaching, many coaches felt the coachee alone needed to prepare for meetings. But we've learned that doesn't work. For the process to have lasting benefits, the coach must prepare for meetings and be 100 percent invested in them. Otherwise, the coachee misses out on an opportunity to grow.

Similarly, if the coachee does not follow through and complete their commitments, the follow-up is an opportunity for the coach to explore why that happened. What obstacles prevented their coachee from meeting their obligations? How can they get around those obstacles in the future? How can we recalibrate our commitment to ensure we make some progress before our next meeting? If the coachee fails for some reason, the coach can still hold them accountable, reinforce the importance of the coachee's commitment, and enforce the coachee's consequence model. Without that, the coachee shrugs and assumes they can get away with continuing to underperform. They assume no one really cares whether they put in the extra work.

If the coachee *is* successful but the coach postpones the meeting or arrives at it distracted, the coach misses an opportunity to recognize the coachee's effort and commitment. That recognition is what truly unites the coach and coachee, and a distracted coach misses the chance to come together with their charge for a common victory. When the coach misses or de-prioritizes follow-up, they are saying that the coachee's commitment wasn't that valuable. The coach says, "I have more pressing matters on my plate."

In Chapter 1, I talked about the sales manager who didn't enforce standards for his staff but maintained a strict 10:00 p.m. curfew for his teenage daughter. When I asked him about that, he realized that he would never negotiate that curfew with his daughter yet he was willing to let his sales staff work without focus, follow-up, and accountability. He had a high standard for his family, but he allowed his staff to negotiate the standard. Once he stopped negotiating standards with his workers and employed rigorous follow-up to ensure the standards were met, his store's sales skyrocketed, and he became one of the company's top managers.

Follow-up is everything. It's a link in the chain that can't be weak, or the whole process will collapse. If it's not done properly and consistently, you lose trust, ownership, and accountability. You nullify all the steps that preceded it. You have spent all that time and energy to intensely connect and commit to a very concentrated, focused area, and your coachee has put in a lot of time and energy under your guidance and prompting. If you suddenly cancel on them or don't follow through with focus and energy, how likely will it be that they will want to invest in the next conversation? It's like silent quitting. They won't participate in future endeavors at the same level they would have invested if their coach had followed up. They thought their coach was committed but now it appears they weren't.

Under the old coaching paradigm, the boss tells the team member what to do, and the team member executes that directive. But they do it without the commitment and sense of ownership of someone being coached under this new system. So, when I hear old-school bosses complaining that they are having trouble coaching someone, I always ask, "As a coach, how committed are you to the process? What level of energy and intensity are you bringing to the coaching process?" If you expect a certain level of enthusiasm and commitment from your team members, you must model that as a coach. Your focus and fire have to match what you expect from your coachee. They won't give you that level of urgency if you don't show the same or higher level of urgency yourself.

PREPARATION IS KEY

Before a follow-up meeting, it's critical that the coach review their notes so they have a firm understanding of what the coachee committed to and what they used for success metrics.

When the meeting starts, your initial goal is to make the coachee feel comfortable. You might ask in a general way about how they are doing, if they had a good weekend, or how they are feeling. You check in on the person. You show that you care about them on a personal level, too. After a few minutes, you can get down to business and ask the coachee to recap what their commitment was and what action steps they took.

The coach needs to be prepared for different conversations that might flow out of that exchange. In most cases, the coaches will hear that the coachee either met their commitment or they didn't. You have to be ready to respond to either answer.

If they failed, you have to explore why. Why was the commitment not met? You're better off to be transparent and open right away. What challenges prevented them from meeting their commitment? You want to stay pretty broad and allow them to fill you in on their experience. Their response likely will give you an opportunity to dig a little deeper. For instance, they might say they got busy during the week and could not make the extra calls they committed to. What kept them so busy? How can we prioritize these commitments, which during the commitment stage you added to your schedule? You challenge them to think differently. Everyone is busy these days, so the question is how do we make these calls a priority next week? Sometimes the conversation can drill down into motivation. Ask the coachee, "How did you feel when you didn't hit your goal?" How do they react? Are they indifferent? Or are they clearly disappointed? If they are disappointed, ask how they can use that emotion in the future to meet their commitment. Are they going to have the same determination next week and miss their goals again, or is there something they could do differently to meet those commitments?

If the failure is persistent, the coach needs to backtrack and rhetorically go through the coachee's commitment and recount why it's important. Why did the two of you agree that this was the important thing they could focus on? Why is it important to your business and your outcomes? Why is it important to you? You want to get everything out of them and almost relive the creation stage. Recognize their contribution to this point but point out their inability to follow through. "Is this the wrong focus and commitment? Or is there a challenge going on that's holding you back from doing the things you say you want to achieve?" In other words, is this the wrong strategy or do they lack the commitment or intensity to put it in place? If that's the case, ask them what you, their coach, can do to help them gain the intensity they need.

If they succeeded, congratulate them and recognize the effort it took to meet their commitment. How did it feel to accomplish this? What was the biggest challenge you had to overcome? You reinforce that there will always be obstacles but recognize that they successfully hurdled those obstacles. Revel in that a bit. Then you want to get an assessment: How easy or hard was it for you to accomplish? Is it something you will be able to do consistently from week to week? Most people won't say the job was easy, but after the coachee successfully meets their commitments for a few weeks running, the coach typically will ask, "Do you feel you want to add more?"

A coach should always have a good recognition system, and that starts with understanding how their coachee likes to be recognized. It's not always about the results but their commitment to the process. Some like to be recognized for their improved numbers while some are motivated by money or competition. If they're competitive, you might say, "Wow. Amazing effort. You hit your focus item, and it makes you number one on the team. How does that feel?" Some people are self-motivated, but that's rare. Most people need to be motivated, so a key part of the coaching cycle in follow-up is knowing what motivates them so you can give them a little extra gas in the tank they'll need to get through the next commitment and stage. You've got to rev them up. "Next time I see you, we should be able to recognize you for hitting this number again." You're programming in certain behaviors or habits, creating a dopamine response each time they get recognized. They anticipate that feeling. You can see it when they come into a coaching meeting, and their shoulders are higher and there is an air of anticipation about them. They've got good news, and they know they are going to be recognized.

CONTINUOUS IMPROVEMENT THAT COMPOUNDS

Tiger Woods was arguably the best golfer in the world when he decided he needed to improve his swing. In 1997, while working with coach Butch Harmon, Woods made significant alterations to his swing to improve his power and efficiency while reducing body stress. While initially his golf scores increased, the changes soon allowed Woods to have a breakthrough year. He won the Masters by a record margin and solidified his reputation as golf's most dominant player.

Michael Jordan was another high-level athlete who wasn't satisfied with the status quo. He was always looking for ways to get better, whether it was through better conditioning, meditation, or better mental preparation.

In many organizations, people don't go for continuous improvement like that. They do what's comfortable. They go for continuous maintenance or continuous status quo. They repeat the same goals and behaviors. You see this at the gym as well. Ninety percent of the people there do the same workouts they've done in the past with the same level of energy and intensity. They're maintaining, but they aren't growing or improving.

To improve, you have to do something different. You have to increase the intensity level.

In coaching, that point occurs after your coachee has established a cadence of successfully fulfilling their commitments. Typically, the next level up for someone you are coaching would occur every ninety days or so. They've demonstrated some discipline, achieved some outcomes, and are increasingly comfortable with the process. Still, you must be careful not to push too hard too fast or threaten to undercut your progress. Some people think they can continuously elevate, elevate, elevate. You see that in new runners, for example. Once they get used to the training, they love it so much that they add too many miles too quickly and get burned out or injured. It's crucial that the coachee learns to crawl and then to walk before they start running. You can't go from crawling consistently with discipline and standards and then just break into a sprint. So you crawl for a time, then you walk till you're comfortable walking, and then you begin to jog. There is nothing worse than developing a good system and then becoming overwhelmed and falling back.

When people trust that there will be regular follow-up with their coach, from an accountability standpoint and a recognition one as well, certain benefits accrue. There is a compounding effect, which is when small behaviors repeated over time add up to a massive win. For example, I had a client who was a salesperson who estimated that he converted 5 percent to 10 percent of his sales calls. With that in mind, he aimed to increase his call volume by ten calls a day, or fifty a week. That didn't sound like a lot, but if you keep it up for a month, you are making 200 more calls, and over the year it amounts to 2,400 calls. He calculated that if he were to keep that pace going, he would double or triple his annual income. Talk about a motivator! My coachee began to think differently about adopting small behaviors and doing them consistently.

The problem is that most people won't do those small behaviors consistently. They do them for a time but they taper off as they lose sight of this crucial compounding effect. This is why it makes sense for coachees to build these standards into their routines and ensure the work is consistently completed and measured. Over time, you develop a consistent rhythm and start to see that compounding effect. This consistency is what we call a growth habit strategy. You determine the one or two behaviors that give you the highest return on your desired outcome, and you build them into your regular cadence. If we go back to the weight-loss analogy, diet management and exercise are the two crucial behaviors, so you create a system for consistently adhering to the standards, tracking your behaviors, and holding yourself accountable. As we mentioned earlier, if it's only one or two things, you can focus on them 100 percent, whereas if you add too many things, your focus gets muddled and you can't get 100 percent on any of your standards.

CLARITY AND ALIGNMENT

Another key piece of the follow-up is confirming alignment. By that, I mean it's vital that you review your original goals, confirming that those are still crucial to your success, and then building it into the coachee's schedule. Ask your coachee, "Are these still the right things we should focus on? Are you comfortable adding these action steps to your daily and weekly workload?" Alignment allows you to maintain clarity and confirmation. Moreover, the easiest way to stay aligned is by asking your coachee, "Are we on the same page? Is there anything we need to tweak?" This is another reason why the coach–coachee relationship is so critical. If you don't have that level of transparency, you can't have clarity. If you don't have clarity it's hard to have alignment. The coachee will tell you what you want to hear, not what you need to hear.

Many people aren't accustomed to having their leader ask for clarity. They're used to having someone accept their surface-level response. But a good coach isn't satisfied with that. They will dig deeper, and if the coachee is being disingenuous, the coach's questions will expose that. For example, I'm a big "show me" kind of guy. When I'm coaching someone, and they reassure me that they met their commitment, I'll say, "Great! Show me the numbers you compiled. Let's crack open that call log. I'm eager to see how you managed to schedule these extra calls." This has caught more than a few people by surprise. They've never had a boss who took it a step further and asked for evidence of their coachee's extra work.

"You didn't think I was going to ask how you did it?" I'll reply.

"Well, no one's ever asked before," they'll admit.

"Trust me," I'll reply. "I'll always ask. How do we know it's happened if you can't show me?"

This isn't an attempt to embarrass them or harass them. It's how you hold people accountable. If they fail to meet their commitment, you don't respond with recriminations. Instead, you need to find out what got in the way and how they will manage that obstacle in the future. They come to understand that their coach really wants them to succeed and isn't going to be satisfied hearing empty reassurances. The two of you are in this together. Your coach is keeping up their end of the bargain by paying close attention to your efforts. You need to uphold your end of the bargain by meeting your commitments and finding routes around the roadblocks in your way. Together, you celebrate those successes in the follow-up phase of your coaching.

This accountability framework works for both the coach and the coachee. We've talked about how the coachee can be held accountable, but what about the coach? Is the coach arriving at the follow-up meetings prepared? Are they cognizant of what the coachee promised to do and are they asking to see the evidence those promises were kept? Has the coach done everything in their power to create an accountable environment? Does the coach feel the same sense of ownership in this process that the coachee does? Good coaches, once they've established an accountability framework, don't have to ask their coachees to "show me" proof of their commitment. The coachees come to their follow-up with all the data the coach might need. Software tools like Trello or Asana are a great way to track progress.

TRANSACTIONAL VERSUS
TRANSFORMATIONAL FOLLOW-UP

You'll likely damage your relationship if you, as a coach, come into a follow-up meeting and just ask about the nuts and bolts of the coachee's activity. "Did you do what you said you were going to do, or didn't you? Just give me a yes or no. How many additional calls did you make? Show me the log. How many additional sales?" It's all very cold, very black-and-white, and it's harmful.

A transformational follow-up starts with making the coachee comfortable. Whether they met their obligations or didn't, you're still their coach, and you're still involved in the process. You still want them to succeed, and you have oceans of patience. This doesn't mean you're soft, but it does mean you're transparent and direct. You don't want to create an emotional response by elevating your tone and saying, "Well why didn't you get this thing done?" instead of "Help me understand why you didn't get this thing done." You must choose your words carefully, but you also need to manage your tone. The exact same statement can sound curious (good) or it could sound intrusive (harmful). Check your body language as well. Be sensitive to the level of tension in the room. Ask questions calmly and in a supportive manner while remembering that you are holding your coachee accountable to take the actions they determined necessary for them to improve. If a coach is having a virtual coaching session, they can record the session and review it later with an eye for tone, speed, body language, and general responses. What seemed to work well? What could the coach have done differently to achieve better results?

In their 2004 book *How Full Is Your Bucket?* authors Tom Rath and Donald O. Clifton explore the idea of a metaphorical bucket that represents one's emotional well-being.[31] Positive actions and interactions with others fill our bucket—bringing happiness and fulfillment—while negative actions and experiences empty our bucket, leaving us depleted and unhappy.

---

31   Tom Rath and Donald O. Clifton, *How Full Is Your Bucket?* (Gallup Press, 2004), 25.

As their coach, ask yourself, "Did I fill their bucket or take from their bucket?" In other words, in this follow-up scenario, did I help support their growth or did my disappointment or apparent anger take from their growth? If you frustrate the process rather than influence it, you might take people off track and make them less receptive to future feedback.

CHAPTER 7 GROWTH REFLECTION QUESTIONS AND ACTIVITIES

1. How can you better prepare for the follow-up process and prepare for recognition or reinforcement?
2. How do you like to give recognition to others? How could you improve that aspect in your role as a leader and coach?
3. List five benefits of holding people more accountable through strict follow-up. How do your coachee and the people around them benefit?

8

SYSTEMATIZATION

HOW TO STAY F.I.T. WITH FREQUENCY, INTENSITY, AND TECHNIQUE

"No matter how good you get you can always get better, and that's the exciting part."

—TIGER WOODS

Till now, the coaching process has been about plowing new ground—making discoveries, building awareness, establishing focus and commitment, and following up on the coachee's project on the things they committed to doing. We've even taken measures to ensure continuous, ongoing improvement. These elements comprise the full arc of the coaching process, but your work as a coach doesn't end there. Now it's time to systemize the process so you can iterate and help your coachees continue to grow and improve as they face new challenges that call for ongoing awareness, focus, commitment, and follow-up.

Borrowing from Mark Sanborn's F.I.T. technique in his book *The Potential Principle: A Proven System for Closing the Gap Between How Good You Are and How Good You Could Be*, the key elements of systematization and continuous improvement are frequency, intensity, and technique. Frequency refers to how often you work with each coachee, intensity measures the level of focus and commitment, and technique encompasses the methods you use to measure progress and ensure continuous improvement.[32] Again, the example of weight loss helps us visualize these elements. As part of your weight-loss program, you've decided to work out three times a week for an hour. Is that frequent enough, or should you work out five times a week to accomplish your weight-loss goal? During those workouts, are you elevating your heart rate high enough? You're at 70 percent of your maximum heart rate on average but should your effort be more intense—say 80 percent of your max? Finally, what methods are you using in your exercise? Your technique now might be to run two days a week and lift weights on the third day. Is running the right cardiovascular exercise for you or should you be swimming or riding a bike to achieve that 80 percent maximum heart rate? Adding variety will prevent someone from getting bored or losing focus and intensity.

In a workplace coaching scenario, frequency can refer to how often you meet with your coachee and for how long. It can also refer to the frequency of some of the coachee's actions. For instance, your coachee has determined that they need to make 20 percent more calls each week to reach their sales goal. Is that the right frequency?

Intensity is literally the level of work a coachee is willing to put in. As author David Goggins points out, everyone can do 100 percent more than they typically do.[33] Our mind convinces us to stop because we don't feel comfortable and should rest, but the truth is we have the capacity for far more intensity. If you are intensely committed to the process, you can do more. You must tell yourself you can do more and commit to doing more.

Technique, meanwhile, refers to the methodology your coachee uses to improve. Are they self-reflecting to improve? Are they seeking

---

32   Mark Sanborn, *The Potential Principle: A Proven System for Closing the Gap Between How Good You Are and How Good You Could Be* (Nelson Books, 2017), 45–46.

33   David Goggins, *Can't Hurt Me: Master Your Mind and Defy the Odds* (Lioncrest Publishing, 2018).

someone inside their circle to help them improve? For example, I've committed to working out for the last twenty years. Could I find a better way to deadlift? I felt there was, so I hired a personal trainer last year, and my form is twenty times better than it was. For twenty years, I worked on my technique alone, but I never connected with the right form until my trainer showed me.

TOOLS FOR SYSTEMATIZATION

The first step in systematization is to review your nonnegotiables or your coaching arrangement and ensure you stick with them. For example, there should always be an agenda for each coaching meeting, and that agenda should always go out twenty-four or thirty-six hours before the meeting. Having an agenda allows the person attending the meeting to be more proactive and prepared. There is always a recap email after every meeting that describes action items. Post-meeting notes drive accountability because they show an alignment between what was said and what was committed. The coach and coachee must be clear on these commitments. Systematization is about getting a commitment on time and cadence for your meetings. Weekly or bimonthly? For an hour or thirty minutes? You want a systemized cadence so you can develop a rhythm. It's at a time that is convenient for both parties, and it's on each person's calendar. Are you meeting in person or using a videoconferencing system like Zoom or Google Meets?

Keep things simple and effective. Some coaches use programs like Trello, Asana, or some other platform to keep things on track, but not everyone needs that level of complexity. The simpler your system, the easier it is to execute. You will still need a scorecard to track progress, but that scorecard should be as simple as the jumbotron at the ballpark—relevant stats only.

It's critical that each meeting has a written agenda. One standing item will be a recap of the last conversation and the one or two action items that emerged from that meeting. Some coaches like to add their questions to the agenda, but others would rather pose those questions in person so they can see the coachee's surface-level response. Sometimes those reactions are revealing.

When working with CEOs and executives, I usually send them the questions ahead of time. You want them to have time to prepare their answers. However, I also like to keep some secondary follow-up questions tucked away in my back pocket for the face-to-face meeting. Asking questions live tends to encourage truer answers, especially when you are digging deeper throughout the process.

Post-call notes are vital because they capture the whole conversation. They reflect what you've agreed and should be broken down by responses to specific questions. This gives the coachee an opportunity to take a second run at a question; in private and after reflection, they may be able to offer additional insights. You should also have a parking lot for items that you and the coachee will address in the future. The note should also include action items you've agreed to and a timeline for when those will be completed and by whom. The post-call notes should also itemize topics for the next call. This will serve as a start on the next meeting's agenda.

Sometimes coaches withhold questions because they want to catch the coachee off guard and get them to make a realization. For example, say I'm coaching an executive, and I really want this leader to realize they need a better leadership development program for their executive team. So I might ask him, "What programs are you currently working on that are focused on developing your leadership team?"

"Oh, we're working on this, that, and the other thing," the CEO says.

"Great! Which of those programs are you personally involved in?"

A lot of times they aren't involved in any of them. They are just facilitating the training for others. But as their coach, it's clear to me that they would benefit from these programs as well. So I'll ask them what the advantages would be if they *were* involved. I don't give them that question ahead of time because I don't want a planned answer but an honest one. In that sense, the question creates a bit of vulnerability and perhaps a realization on the leader's part that, yeah, I might benefit from these programs, too. When that happens, you need to recognize them for their vulnerability and for being open and honest. This makes them more comfortable, and it sends the signal that we're here to have real conversations, not fake ones. It gives you an opportunity to say, "Great response! I think pulling this plan together with you involved will help you better connect with your leaders and give you insight into how those programs are coming along."

You're trying to recognize them for being vulnerable and open to honesty. This makes them more willing to be forthright in future conversations about other questions, and it reconfirms that your meetings are in a private space.

CHAPTER 8 GROWTH REFLECTION QUESTIONS AND ACTIVITIES

1. Identify an area where you could improve personally using the F.I.T. technique of frequency, intensity, and technique.
2. Now identify where someone you coach could benefit from the F.I.T. technique. Use guiding questions to make them self-aware of where they could improve without telling them.

LEADING UP, ACROSS, AND DOWN

COACHING SKILLS HELP WITH MANY RELATIONSHIPS

"Emerging leaders need mentors to guide them, but they also need a network of peers to reassure them that they are not on the path alone."

—ALYSE NELSON

In a traditional coaching setting, leaders guide the people they supervise. Although the process is collaborative, open, and honest, it still has a hierarchical dynamic. In most instances, the coach outranks the coachee.

Does this mean a coach can't influence their peers or even their own supervisors? Not at all. They can, but the process starts with the same discovery and awareness questions the coach asks their coachees, such as, "How can I influence my peers when I don't have a position over them?" This question (and ones like it) force a deeper conversation that helps influence the direction of the strategy. Instead of saying, "I think you should do this," you might say, "Have you thought about doing it this way?" or "How would you approach solving this?" or "Is this something you've tackled with your team?" You're changing your approach to guiding the conversation.

LEADING ACROSS

Leading up and leading across are more challenging than leading down. But there are ways to do it successfully. For instance, say a peer in another division is struggling to get performance out of their team. It might be that the leader isn't familiar with the team's KPIs or their team meetings are out of cadence. The easy thing would be for you to tell your peer, "I think you need to define your KPIs and get a closer cadence with your meetings." However, your peer's reaction might be, "Well, who do you think *you* are? You're not my boss!" They may not say this but that's how they will feel.

You'll get a better reaction if you say, "Tell me a little about the performance of your team. How do you guys look at KPIs in your division?" or "What are some of the goals you're working with your team members on?" They might give you some surface-level response, and if that happens, you can dig a little deeper.

"How do you make it specific for them?"

"I don't know if it's specific enough."

"Well, how would it affect the performance of the team if they *were* more specific?"

You're still semi-coaching them, but it's a co-created conversation. That's the most important element of a peer-to-peer coaching conversation. If you see there is a problem with the cadence of your peer's team meetings, you might ask a question almost like you're asking *them* for advice. "I'm not sure our team has the right meeting cadence. How often do you meet with *your* team? What's your biggest challenge in ensuring those meetings are consistent? What's some feedback you can give me to make those meetings more effective?" You're trying to get them to open up and see that you want a two-way conversation. It might sound like you're trying to make a friend, but in reality, you're building trust with your peers. When there is trust, there's vulnerability. When there's vulnerability, you have the ability to coach without the title of "coach."

In the same sense, you're inviting the peer to observe with you. You're asking them to take you through their business and explain how they navigate it. Along the way, you make observational assessments and ask questions about those observations. This puts a new lens on their situation. Most people force their own perspective on how they see the world. They have one lens, and you're trying to provide them with another set of lenses.

This approach is similar to the Johari Window, a psychological model designed to help individuals improve their communication skills and relationships. The window is a four-quadrant grid depicting a person's personality and how they are perceived by themselves and others. The Open or Arena quadrant represents information about an individual that is known to them and others, and the Blind Spot quadrant depicts what others know about the individual. The Hidden or Facade quadrant represents what the individual knows about themselves but hasn't shared with others and the Unknown quadrant represents information about the individual that is unknown to them as well as others.

THE JOHARI WINDOW

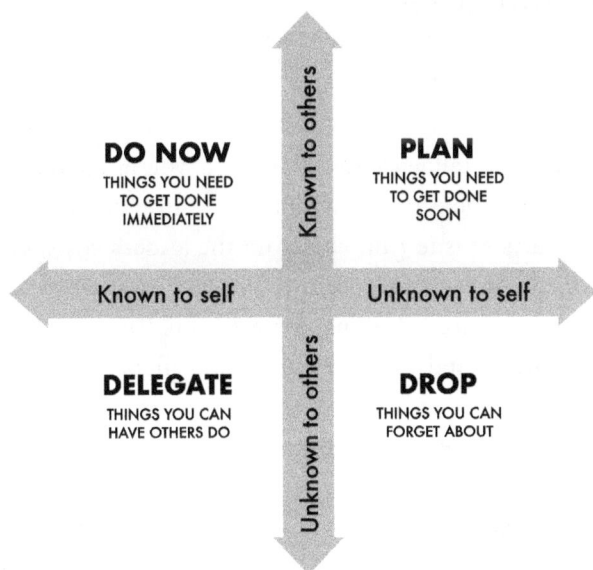

Known to others

DO NOW
THINGS YOU NEED
TO GET DONE
IMMEDIATELY

PLAN
THINGS YOU NEED
TO GET DONE
SOON

Known to self — Unknown to self

Unknown to others

DELEGATE
THINGS YOU CAN
HAVE OTHERS DO

DROP
THINGS YOU CAN
FORGET ABOUT

The theory behind the window is that those who increase the size of their Arena quadrant by sharing information about themselves with others and receiving feedback improve self-awareness, mutual understanding, and better communication. Using that as a backdrop, coaching across uses questions to expand the Arena quadrant and shrink your peer's Blind Spot quadrant. You're not coming out and saying, "Wow. You really have a blind spot about the importance of follow-up, right?" Instead, you are using questions to help them realize this blind spot for themselves.

In some circumstances, your peer-to-peer coaching might be directed at encouraging teams to collaborate. We recently worked with a company where two different teams came together and each team had its own set of goals. They met, shared their goals, and then left. They never asked themselves, "What's the common goal that links our two divisions?" Instead, it was as if they were jockeying for position, trying to assert that their goals and priorities were more important than the other team's. They needed some coaching to understand that they were more likely to succeed if they found some mutually beneficial common ground to work from. This is a huge opportunity for peer coaching and alignment in collaboration.

LEADING UP

When you want to influence someone above you in the hierarchy, it's crucial to have an objective going into the conversation. Most of the time, your purpose is to gain clarity on the leader's goals, objectives, and alignment. Your best opportunity to lead up is when the leader you want to influence is leading down to you. They have questions about performance updates, for example, and after answering, you ask clarifying questions and basic curiosity questions, such as "Where is this taking us?" You're not challenging the strategy; you just want to understand it better.

In seeking clarity from someone above you in the hierarchy, try to determine the rationale or purpose behind the steps being considered.

Why was this particular strategy selected? Why was it considered the most important? What role does this strategy play in our overall, long-term success? You want the leader's perspective on the strategy; you need that to get better clarity for yourself. What part of this strategy should we be most urgent about? What part of this strategy is your favorite part? If we were to revise the strategy, is there anything you would have done differently? Again, you're not challenging the boss's decisions. You just want them to open up about the decisions. **Being curious when leading up is a superpower!**

When people aren't brought into a strategy, they often think the company is saying NO to something. But when we're communicating and connecting—seeking clarity—it's not about NO, it's about KNOW. You understand more by asking more.

In sales training, we talk about how to turn a NO into KNOW. People who seem to be saying NO don't know enough to say yes or don't see enough value to say yes. So you might need to do some digging to have them understand why this is a YES product or opportunity for them. It's about understanding what they know and why—what's driving their decision?—and using a don't-stop-at-no attitude and using questions to learn more. The more you learn and educate, the more they will KNOW and more likely they are to say yes. When we equip people with information and value, they have a more clear decision-making process. They might still say no, but it's an educated no instead of a no that comes from uncertainty or misperceptions.

Clarity is one benefit from these conversations with your boss, but there are other benefits as well. There's a Chinese proverb:

"THOSE WHO DRINK THE WATER MUST REMEMBER THOSE WHO DUG THE WELL."

In your conversations with your boss, it's important to respect the role they played in digging the well. When you have that gratitude, your questions can veer into your boss's professional history and accomplishments. You're not simply trying to suck up to them but instead to identify how they got to where they're at and learn their professional path so you can follow it. In this sense, leading up is about you being a potential successor for your boss. The closer your connection and understanding of who they are and how they achieved their position, the more open and trusting your boss will be to your feedback. If you get a strong enough relationship, they may eventually come to you for feedback on their activities as a leader.

Leading up can also occur when you're being proactive about issues. For example, say you're a new leader and your team had a weak first quarter. Is this an opportunity to lead up?

Being proactive is always a good strategy. You want to recognize the issue and be accountable. You can start by acknowledging the poor first-quarter performance and ask, "Can I get some time with you to get your insight into how we could do things differently in the second quarter?" You're being forthright and proactive. You're not making excuses, and you're holding yourself accountable. You're also sending the message that you are open to learning, and your boss will appreciate that. Moreover, you're not waiting for the boss to initiate the discussion and set the terms. You're doing that.

A crucial piece of this is your understanding of what makes this leader tick. What are their key priorities? What motivates them? What are they focused on right now? When you know that, you can incorporate those interests into your conversation with them. You are meeting with them to address their priorities while also looking for help with yours. You also want to be aware of their strengths and use opportunities to acknowledge those strengths. (Flattery *does* help.) So, for instance, you might say, "You do an amazing job planning strategies, and I'd like to bring our strategy to you and get your insight." Try to get their time and focus by identifying their strengths and looking for ways to capitalize on those strengths so you both can benefit from them. If you win, they win.

If the leader knows you care about the conversation and are seeking more of the KNOW, they're more open to sharing their perspective on where the strategy comes from. Sharing it gives the leader a better perspective on the strategy itself because they have to explain it. That's why when someone takes an idea and it gets acknowledged by people, the more questions we ask about it force the person to refine the idea and add more detail, which gives a better understanding. It's a big challenge. Many middle managers put on a mask and ask, "What does my boss want to hear today?" Someone who knows how to lead understands their leader's history, their track record with other companies, and can tap into those things. I did that a lot when I was in middle management. I would find out their history—where they grew up, what sports they played, and where they used to work—and I would say, "I know you used to work at XYZ company. Is there anything you used to do that would solve the problem I'm facing right now?" They would recognize that you tapped into their past and they will be happy to share.

Leading up is like a piggy bank; the more "face time" you get leading up, the more equity you build with that leader. They value the curiosity you bring because it helps them flesh out their own thought process.

Learning about the leaders and their personal history is something that you have to work on over time. Find out where they grew up, what their hobbies are, and where they used to work. The more you know, the more you can speak to it. You do this out of curiosity and genuinely wanting to build a relationship. It's not about trying to manipulate them but about knowing them better. You can lead at all levels if you manage the relationship first. Find out everything about everybody. It's more than asking, "Why is Bob a good account manager?" It's more about asking "Who is Bob? What is Bob's family like? What does Bob do in his spare time? How can I leverage some of those pieces to build a relationship so Bob can trust me?" When we meet people and we work with people over time, we're always consistently gauging "Can I trust this person or not?" We always reinforce that trust or relationship. The three things that people talk about most are their job, family, and pastime. So I try to hit all three to better understand the person as a whole versus who they are at work.

MENDING STRAINED RELATIONS

When leading up or across, you may encounter situations where you need to heal a past relationship that got off on the wrong foot or was at one point damaged by conflict. The first step in repairing them is acknowledging that you do, indeed, want a better relationship. If the two parties don't want to repair it, it will never be fixed.

MORE RELATIONSHIPS HAVE BEEN ENDED BY WHAT WASN'T SAID THAN BY WHAT WAS SAID.

So some people who go head-to-head have this silent dismissal of the other person and vow to never interact with them again if they can help it. So then the conflict isn't about a collision between two angry people but instead is about avoidance. People fear conflict. They fear the outcomes of conflict and they fear what someone is going to say. In my experience, though, when you get those people together and get them to communicate and connect, they realize how small many of their original issues were. If you take a structured approach to just sitting down and addressing the issue without placing blame, you can make significant changes. The first step is to find common goals and work together to achieve a win-win.

Whether you are leading down, across, or up, relationships play a massive role in all areas. How are we sharing our perspectives with people? Regarding the Johari Window, how big are we making our Open quadrant and how are we inviting people to help us shrink our Blind Spots? Moreover, how strong is your relationship with people unlike you? People have good relationships with those who are just like them.

How well can you adapt your style to be able to relate to people of all groups and personalities? The key distinction here is this: somebody is always trying to win, but they're not trying to win together. So leading up, down, and across is about finding mutually beneficial outcomes. A critical piece of leading at all levels is establishing and articulating what a common win looks like.

DIFFICULT CONVERSATIONS

What do we mean by difficult conversations? They could be any number of things. Maybe you have a disagreement with a coworker and it's left you both feeling uncomfortable. You may have to sit down with that person and talk about your differences, how to resolve them, and how to avoid them in the future. It could also be that your coachee has dropped the ball on something they promised to do, and you need to point it out to them. It could be you have to deliver the news to a client that their product has been delayed.

Whatever the reason, suffice it to say that we don't like having difficult conversations, and we tend to avoid them like the plague. That, of course, is not the right answer. When we avoid difficult conversations, issues escalate, resentment grows, there is disengagement, lost productivity, and damage to your work culture. The right answer is to prepare for difficult conversations and manage them to ensure they go as smoothly as possible. There are ways to have these conversations that are productive and maintain your relationships. Here are a few things to keep in mind:

- Shift to the positive. A difficult conversation typically involves delivering discomforting news, so it's vital to present it in a positive light. If you deliver a performance evaluation to someone who must improve, present it as an opportunity to improve.
- Plan what you'll say. I don't mean you should write out a speech and deliver it; that won't sound natural. Jot down some bullet points, focus on staying calm and even-tempered, and lead a casual con-

versation. Go into the conversation with planned intent. What is your desired outcome?

- Look at it from their perspective. You must acknowledge the other person's viewpoint, and if you don't know it, ask about it. Ensure the other person understands that you truly want to see the issue from their side. Look for common ground.
- Be considerate. In addition to staying calm and pleasant, it's vital that you approach the conversation with an authentic interest in clearing the air. Try to maintain a slow, casual pace. At the same time, be unapologetically clear and direct with your statements. Refrain from judgment or assumption.
- Focus on being experience-based. Again, be kind and direct. Avoid opinions and feelings; feelings aren't facts. Describe how you perceive the impact and your vision for a resolution. Ask open-ended questions. Question for clarity and understanding, not for power or control.

We use a worksheet that helps people navigate difficult conversations. The idea is to help you focus on an outcome, not a solution. So, going into that challenging talk, jot down answers to a few key questions:

- What would be my ideal outcome for this conversation?
- How does that outcome allow both parties to have input that is valued and heard?
- How does that outcome demonstrate my openness to new perspectives?

From these answers, you can construct a rough script for the conversation. While you're not expected to write a speech and present that speech, it does help to have some talking points around the following prompts:

- "I want to talk to you about (a specific situation) from (a specific date)."

- "I noticed (specific observations about the situation and not the person)."
- "I feel that (explain the specific impact of the situation)."
- "I value your perspective and would really appreciate your point of view. What are your thoughts on this?"

Done well, a difficult conversation builds trust, increases awareness, and improves collaboration. Think about that emotional bank account we discussed earlier. If you already have a relationship with the person, then you should have deposited some emotional equity in the other person's piggy bank by previously being an active listener and communicating with them with empathy, kindness, consistency, integrity, and clarity. You've made a lot of deposits and now you must make a withdrawal—by asking them to change their behavior or to hear some potentially troubling feedback.

Stephen Covey once said,

"TWO PEOPLE CAN SEE THE SAME THING, DISAGREE, AND YET BOTH BE RIGHT. IT'S NOT LOGICAL; IT'S PSYCHOLOGICAL."[34]

Remember that you should remain flexible and work to build greater connections and understanding from the other person. Teams that get great at navigating difficult conversations go farther and move quickly.

---

34   Stephen R. Covey, *The 7 Habits of Highly Effective People: Restoring the Character Ethic* (Simon and Schuster, 1989), 27.

CHAPTER 9 GROWTH REFLECTION
QUESTIONS AND ACTIVITIES

1. Write down one relationship you want to influence. Note why you want to have a stronger influence on the relationship. Is this leading up, leading down, or leading across?

2. Identify someone in a peer-to-peer role who you want to better collaborate with and influence.

3. Write down where your relationship is today with this person and where you would like to see it grow.

4. Write down how you want to influence them.

5. Set up your SMART plan. (Remember, it's okay to have plans when influencing a relationship you care about.)

6. Ninety days from now, identify how the relationship has changed and if there were improvements or regression.

10

BRINGING IT ALL TOGETHER

LEARNING HOW TO ASK THE RIGHT QUESTIONS TAKES PRACTICE

"Life takes on meaning when you become motivated, set goals, and charge after them in an unstoppable manner."

—LES BROWN

A basic premise for this book is the notion that a leader's role is not to have an answer to every question. Instead, the leader's role is to ensure all the right questions are posed, and accurate answers emerge from those questions. If you accept that premise, then you also should understand that asking questions helps leaders build the trust, empathy, openness, and vulnerability that helps their team members stretch, grow, and become less dependent on their leader and more confident in solving problems on their own. You also understand that asking good questions isn't effective unless you're willing to listen and learn from what you hear. You want your questions to draw out the best, most relevant thinking of your team members, and it's crucial that you place value on all responses as you and your team work through your challenges.

If you are genuinely curious about what your team members think and show appreciation for their answers, they will in turn believe that you value them. This is incredibly empowering and generates even deeper thinking, better problem-solving, and more open discussion. Start with questions. Don't start with your own conclusions and ask for any contrary views; you're almost certain to get either blank expressions or sycophantic nods of agreement. *Sounds good, boss. Let's do it your way.* That is a surefire way to ensure people have little commitment to the solution or might even try to sabotage it.

You don't want that. While some leaders are content with being frantic firefighters—hearing about every flare-up, issuing directives, and allocating resources—others are more interested in enabling the leadership abilities of their team members. Asking questions helps you do that. More precisely, a leader who asks questions enables others to develop *themselves* as leaders. Skillfully using questions is one of the most profound ways leaders create an environment for others to develop critical thinking skills. It gives team members the crucial experience they need to solve problems and hold themselves accountable for the solution.

Remember that as a leader, you are not expected to have an innate ability to ask the right questions at the right time. You have to learn, and you have to practice. Developing the habit of posing questions will take some time and require a conscious, purposeful effort. You'll have to break the habit you've likely formed of hearing problems and proposing solutions. By changing the paradigm for how you interact with your team members, you're not just growing other members of your team; you are growing yourself. Think again about that personal trainer. That person didn't build your strength and cardiovascular capacity by doing your workouts. You did the workouts. You did the grunting and sweating. You got in shape by learning and applying what your trainer suggested. You can be your team members' personal coach.

Inviting them to answer questions compels them to refine their ideas beyond the surface level or the quick responses. That's a huge development opportunity. You get better answers, better execution, more ownership, and more confident employees. If you're always telling people what to do, it can send the message that you don't trust them to think independently. That creates more dependent thinkers, which creates more headaches for you, their leader, and limits the scope of possible solutions. Asking questions spurs the exchange of ideas and fuels innovation. It can also minimize business risk by revealing potential pitfalls.

Asking questions, particularly during the Discovery phase, is like casting a fishing net. When you haul in your nets, you may have six or seven different chunks of information that you can utilize in coaching your team members. You won't want to act on all seven chunks at once—that would distort the conversation and dilute the focus—but you'll have that information for later as you guide your team's development. You can even use your team to formulate the right questions. This brings them along on the journey of solving big problems and allows them to see the path to the right solution. They asked the right questions and found evidence, and all the diverse viewpoints led to the best answer.

QUESTIONS AND EMOTIONAL INTELLIGENCE

Researchers at Harvard have found that asking questions improves our emotional intelligence.[35] This, in turn, makes us better questioners, creating a virtuous cycle. Asking questions allows us to achieve both of the two major goals of conversation: information exchange (learning) and impression management (liking). People who ask more questions in a conversation are better liked by the conversation partners than those who ask fewer questions. Questioners naturally got to know their partners better and could anticipate their likes and dislikes. Speed daters who ask more questions are more likely to be asked to go on a second date. Questions even pay off during job interviews, when you are ostensibly there to sell yourself to a potential employer. For an interviewee, asking questions suggests they are competent and helps build rapport with future colleagues. Moreover, those chatting with people who ask a lot of questions don't seem to be aware that it's the other person's seemingly

35 Karen Huang et al., "It Doesn't Hurt to Ask: Question-Asking Increases Liking," *Journal of Personality and Social Psychology* 113, no. 3 (2017): 430–452, https://doi.org/10.1037/pspi0000097.

keen interest in them that makes the questioner so likable. The type, tone, and framing of questions play a big role in how those questions land. When someone feels as though they are the center of attention and that you truly care about what they say, you build a closer bond and connection with that person. This is sometimes why people fall in love with their therapist.

In the Harvard research, scientists learned that the best approach to asking questions depended on whether the conversation was cooperative (the two talkers are working together or striving to learn more about each other) or competitive (one talker tried to squeeze advantageous information out of the other person). They boiled questions down to four main types:

- Introductory. (How are you today?)
- Mirror questions. (I'm good. You?)
- Full-switch questions, which suddenly change the topic.
- Follow-up questions.

Of the four, follow-up questions had the most potency. They indicate the questioner is not only listening but is interested in learning more. This makes their partner feel respected and heard. Follow-up questions tend to flow easily; they don't require special preparation or advance thought but simply spill out in a natural rhythm within the conversation. In fact, carefully structured questions can be dangerous; they can make the other party feel like you're trying to trick them into revealing something and this could make them distrustful of your queries. People are more relaxed and willing to share when you ask casual questions rather than formal questions in an official manner.

The most effective conversations are two-way conversations. First, ask yourself how you tend to communicate and how others communicate with you, and then think about how you might shift those communications from one-way communications to two-way communications. How can you get people to be more involved? How are you delivering information to those people; are you doing it in a competitive way or are you opening the conversation up? Do people realize that you care about the information they're sharing? If it's a one-way conversation with information being "sent down" to you, how can you use questions to create a two-way exchange? To create two-way conversations, everyone needs to be contributing. People can't be competing to sound smarter than the other person.

While coaching conversations should be more cooperative than competitive, competitive conversations are valuable in that they can bring information to the surface. Competitive conversations may have more yes-or-no questions. That's fine, provided you are equipped with the right follow-up question. For example, I was working on a set of questions for a client who provides business development tools to banks. The line of questioning started with a yes-or-no question ("Have you recently added any technologies to your banking system?"). If the answer came back "yes," we would ask what they were and get the information we needed to sell them a product they hadn't recently acquired. If they answered "no," we can ask about their overall experience and pain points so we can introduce solutions. A yes or no confirmation gives you two paths and two opportunities. Competitive conversations are good if you plan ahead to have contingency responses when they say yes or no.

ONE-WAY VS TWO-WAY CONVERSATION

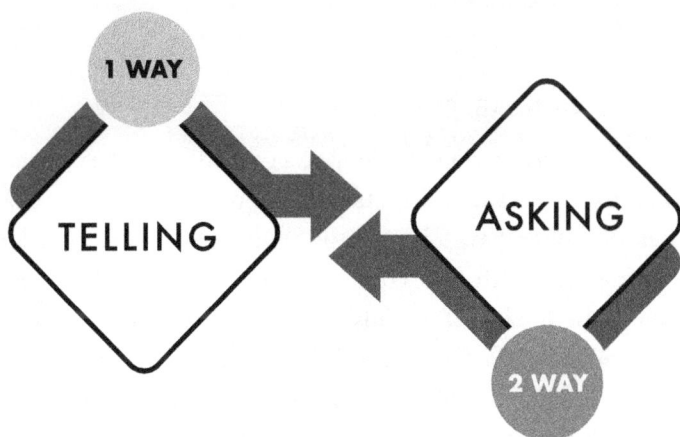

In the Radicle Growth approach, we advise starting with general, overarching questions before narrowing down the scope of your questions. Not all research supports this approach. One study found that people are more willing to reveal sensitive information when questions are asked in decreasing order of intrusiveness. Thus, you might open a conversation by asking, "Have you ever fantasized about hurting someone?" in order to later get an easy answer to a more benign question, such as "Have you ever called in sick when you are feeling just fine?" That might be useful in some circumstances—I'm thinking of how private detective Jake Gittes might ask questions in the movie *Chinatown*—but in most circumstances, we feel it's better to start with shallower questions before moving into the deeper inquiries. One trick that does work is reassuring team members that they can change their answers at any time during your conversation with them; this encourages free thinking and honesty, and people rarely go back and change their initial statements.

I also encourage coaches to have these conversations in a one-on-one setting, and research supports this. In a group setting, a few closed-off or recalcitrant people can cause an entire room to close down. Similarly, when one person starts to open up, others are also likely to talk more. One of the most transformative things we do when running team sessions or workshops is driving questions to the audience to get maximum engagement. It creates a world-class experience.

BEING ACCOUNTABLE IN TEAMS

Any coaching conversation should have a goal. What is the destination you are working toward? The problem is when people get into a change mindset, they often have a laundry list of things they want to achieve. They get together with their coach, and they walk out of the session with ten goals. The law of diminishing returns states that we can only do one or two things at 100 percent. Once we try to do more than that, our effectiveness starts to diminish. If you have two or three goals, you'll likely achieve two or three goals with excellence. However, if you have seven to ten goals, you'll probably fail to achieve any of them at 100 percent. In this sense, *less is more*.

This is why periodization is so important. In Russia, for example, elite athletes would pick one behavior in their sport that they wanted to master, and they would focus on that one thing for 90 or 120 days until they had mastered it. Once that skill was embedded and instinctive, they moved on to the next skill. Meanwhile, athletes practicing ten or fifteen skills failed to master any of them. Periodization was refined in the 1960s by two sports scientists from Russia and Romania, who used the system to bring great success to Eastern Bloc Olympic athletes. The system migrated to the US in the late seventies, although some coaches, including the legendary swim coach James "Doc" Counsilman at the Indiana University, had been using something similar for many years.

You can look at goals as planes that you are trying to land. You can't land multiple planes at once. But if you land them one at a time, you develop skill and confidence as time goes on and you land other planes in the fleet. You don't paralyze yourself by taking on too much. Moreover, you develop confidence in overcoming distractions. Distractions can be the biggest thing that holds us back from growth. But focusing on one or two things gives us a lot of discipline around improving our skills and habits.

Your goals reflect a basic equation, such as going from X to Y by when. Those are the three elements: your starting place, your goal, and your timeline. So, in our weight-loss example, that means you want to go from 185 pounds to 165 pounds by July 1. That's your goal. You plan to reach that goal by exercising for an hour three times a week and limiting your food intake to 1,600 calories a day.

Your goals and measurement system need to be aligned. Tracking progress is only effective if it's reviewed, kept accurate, and carefully followed. I read about a high-level competitive swimmer who trained hard for ten years but had not gotten faster. But was their goal to get faster? Not really. According to the swimmer, they got into the sport so they could lose weight, and they had achieved that.

There is always a direct correlation between what you do and what you get. A lot of growth and development is understanding what you should do to get the best outcomes. Many people focus on the outcomes but not on the activities that will achieve those outcomes. For example, you may have a goal of running a marathon, but you won't get there if you don't train regularly and methodically. You won't develop the stamina and strength you need to run twenty-six miles.

Everything in life is a bet; if I do *this* (make this commitment), I'll get *this* in return. Going back to our weight-loss example, you're betting that if you do that much exercise and limit your calorie intake, you'll drop twenty pounds by July 1. Each week you meet with your coach and hold yourself accountable for your progress. Your scoreboard records your workouts, calorie count, and weight, and you watch those numbers to see if your bet is paying off.

The great thing about this approach is that you eliminate excuses. You are either winning or you're losing. Did I eat under 1,600 calories a day? Yes or no. Did I work out three times last week? Yes or no. There's no debate. You either did or you didn't. If you're winning, you want to know why and how you can do more of it. If you're losing, you want to know why and how you can prevent it and get yourself back on track. The goal in any good coaching conversation is going to be,

---

"HOW DO I MAKE THE GAME SO STRAIGHTFORWARD THAT THERE IS NO REASON FOR EXCUSES?"

The game is either winning or losing.

Just having a coach will increase accountability and drive better urgency, motivation, focus, and clarity. You get out of the idea of being on autopilot. The ecosystem of coaching creates accountability. When people evaluate whether to invest in coaching, they should ask what it would be like to increase everyone's accountability. How would that impact your results or the team's results? Without question, you would get better execution, shorten timelines, and increase everyone's focus—the same way people enjoy better results when they work out with a personal trainer or an athletic coach.

CREATING A SCOREBOARD

In the 1920s and 1930s, researchers investigated the relationship between lighting conditions and worker productivity in the Western Electric Hawthorne Works in Chicago. They learned that regardless of light changes, workers improved their performance when they knew they were being observed or were aware they were part of an experiment.[36]

This came to be called "the Hawthorne effect," which asserts that people will modify their behavior in a positive way if they believe they are being observed or are part of a study. The Hawthorne effect highlights the influence of social and psychological factors on people's performance and productivity and helps explain why having a scoreboard can influence employee behavior in organizational settings.

As Chris McChesney, Sean Covey, and Jim Huling note in their book, *The 4 Disciplines of Execution*, "a big piece of using a scoreboard approach is understanding the difference between 'lag' measures and 'lead' measures."[37] Specifically, the authors state: "While a lag measure tells you if you've achieved the goal, a lead measure tells you if you are likely to achieve the goal." This distinction is essential for creating effective scoreboards, which help teams focus on actionable steps rather than just end results. For weight loss, it might be the bathroom scale. In sports, it's the scoreboard. The lead is the activity that creates the outcome. The lead measure represents the things you do to achieve that goal. They are predictive and influenceable. So, in our example, the lead measures include limiting calories to 1,600 per day and exercising for an hour three days a week.

Part of coaching is making people aware of their activities and the results they get. Most people just don't have measurement systems, and that's a major component of coaching; the better your measurement system, the better you understand the effectiveness of your behaviors.

Tracking your progress requires a scoreboard. Why? As *The 4 Disciplines of Execution* authors note, people play more effectively when they are keep-

---

36 Will Kenton, "Hawthorne Effect Definition: How It Works and Is It Real," Investopedia, July 4, 2024, https://www.investopedia.com/terms/h/hawthorne-effect.asp.

37 Chris McChesney et al., *The 4 Disciplines of Execution: Achieving Your Wildly Important Goals* (Free Press, 2012), 65.

ing score. They are more focused and committed to making progress when they know their success is being measured. Moreover, the coachee—the person pursuing the lag measures—has to "own" their scoreboard. When they take ownership, they are more likely to be committed to it.

An interesting analogy for this dynamic would be to pretend you are watching a basketball game but without any sound or scoreboard. How can you tell if the two teams are keeping score? If the teams *are* keeping score, you can see the players working hard, defending their opponent, and concentrating on getting a good shot. If they *aren't* keeping score, the play becomes looser. Players take wild shots and make risky passes. They don't play defense as hard. There is nothing at stake. For example, consider a high school basketball game between two bitter rivals. A power surge knocks out the scoreboard, but the officials decide to continue the game with scorekeepers recording the score, fouls, etc. by hand. The problem is that the fans can't tell what the score is, how much time is left, and how many fouls have been committed. As a result, they steadily lose interest. Their enthusiasm wanes and the cheering all but vanishes. That's why scoreboards are so important.

In the world of work, the best scoreboards are those that are simple, highly visible, have the right lag and lead measures, and reveal immediately whether we are winning or losing. As *The 4 Disciplines* authors note, maintaining an accurate scoreboard involves a system of accountability between the coach and the coachee; they meet weekly to review last week's commitments, update the scoreboard, and make commitments for the next week. Again, if the coachee doesn't achieve a commitment, the follow-up discussion is not focused on why they failed but on how they are going to avoid failure in the future. There's no room in the discussion to make excuses.

This process works best when it's rigid. It doesn't work under a flimsy or flexible approach. What a coachee reports should be firm. The more flexibility you have the less accountability you have.

MORE ON DIFFICULT CONVERSATIONS

I've never entered a difficult conversation with a question and left without a transformative result. However, if I enter with a statement and try to win or influence my point, I come out feeling emotional and usually further behind than ahead.

Nevertheless, using questions to coach a team member can be challenging when the coachee is resistant. Perhaps the team member is reluctant to open up and keeps the conversation at a surface level. They are not as transparent as they could be. They are underperforming, and they don't have the level of intensity they need to close the gap. They have the right training and knowledge, but they lack focus and concentration. This scenario requires a coach to dig a little deeper and get a little bit tougher in their conversations.

The first step in dealing with this is to isolate the situation. The coachee may be making a lot of excuses, but the coach has to focus on the biggest challenge to the coachee. Is the coachee even aware of this challenge? Their level of self-awareness will dictate the conversation. You have to make them realize there is a problem and how big that problem is. Some team members may not be aware of how big the problem is.

A performance gap analysis will help guide these difficult conversations. You start by revisiting the original objective. What was the coachee's original goal and what are the performance metrics they discussed with their coach? When they reconfirm their goal and metrics, a coach must ask, "Where are we today?" As their coach, you want them to put a dot between where they are and where they should be and measure the distance between those two areas. From there, you can create a conversation that says, "Okay, what does closing that gap look like? And where do we need to modify what we're doing?"

We have a worksheet that helps coaches guide team members through a performance gap analysis. First, the two write down an objective and identify key practices the coachee wants to improve on. The two agree on a "current score" and a "desired score" for that practice based on a scale of 0 to 10. From there, the two fill out a matrix that lists the following:

- Current practice
- Ideal practice
- Performance need

- Performance gap
- Learning objective
- Area of focus

The accompanying graphic gives an example of what that form might look like for a company selling a SaaS platform.

PERFORMANCE GAP ANALYSIS

PRACTICE: DEVELOPER RESOURCES FOCUSED ON NEW FEATURES

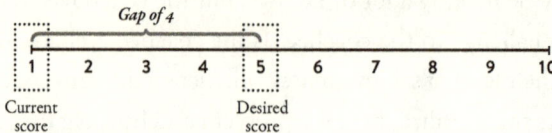

Gap of 4

1   2   3   4   5   6   7   8   9   10

Current score   Desired score

PRACTICE: AVERAGE CUSTOMER SCORE ON INNOVATION

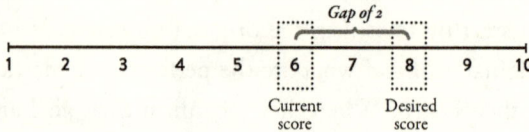

Gap of 2

1   2   3   4   5   6   7   8   9   10

Current score   Desired score

Current Practice	Ideal Practice	Performance Need	Performance Gap	Learning Objective	Area of Focus
Objective: A company wants to be recognized as one of the most innovative SaaS platforms in the industry. They are reviewing their developer resources and sourcing customer feedback on innovation.					
10% of developer resources are focused on new features	50% of developer resources are focused on new features	Additional staff to support research and creation of new features	Capacity	Ensure staffing numbers are meeting deliverables	Team expansion: will hire 2 new developers by end of Q3
Scoring an average of 6/10 on customer feedback in regards to innovation	Scoring an average of 8/10 on customer feedback in regards to innovation	Research various SaaS platforms used in the industry	Capacity	Implement an Innovation Checkpoint for all new features by end of Q3	Research and development

Why do people underperform? Typically, people underperform because they do what's needed at the simplest level because they fear what needs to happen and the intensity required to get there. The accompanying graphic depicts this journey from the Comfort Zone to the Growth Zone. To grow, you have to make your way through the Fear Zone, which is where people lack self-confidence, make excuses, and are affected by others' opinions, and the Learning Zone, which is where you deal with challenges and problems, acquire new skills, and expand your comfort zone. The Growth Zone is where you find purpose, conquer your objectives, and set new goals. The Growth Zone then morphs into a Comfort Zone, and the process of learning and overcoming fear starts all over again.

THE COMFORT ZONE

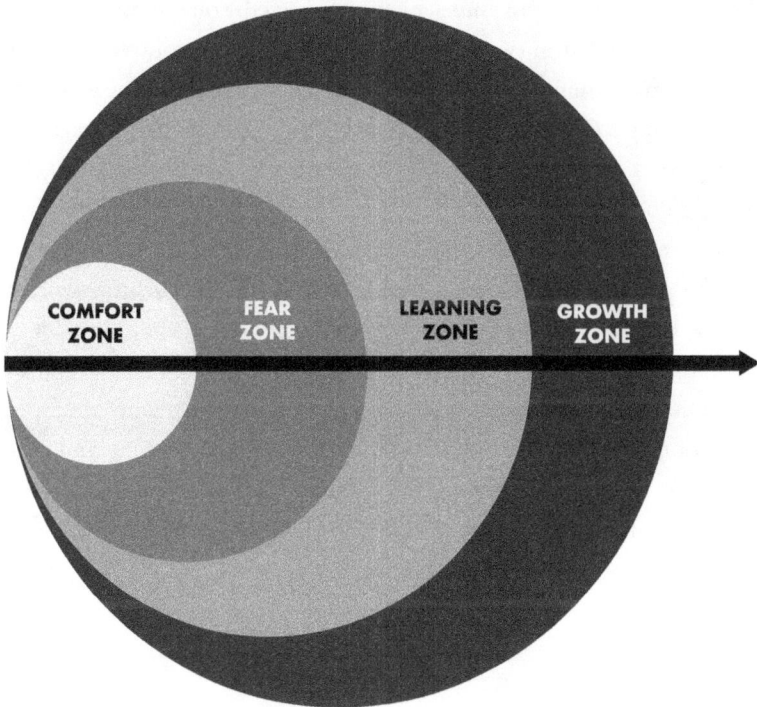

COMFORT ZONE **FEAR ZONE** **LEARNING ZONE** **GROWTH ZONE**

Most people who are in their comfort zone are underperforming. They lack a sense of urgency or accountability. They get defensive about being asked to do more. So, when you compel them into that Fear Zone and make them accountable for dealing with the challenges and problems, they have to acquire new skills. A coach has to help them build that habit and establish a routine. It's not easy, and we shouldn't expect it to be. Nothing that we grow through is easy. But it's about having that relationship between coach and coachee to identify what's needed to get through the Fear and Learning Zones to reach the Growth Zone. You plant the seeds in the Fear Zone, and you reap the harvest in the Growth Zone as the hard work and habitualization carry you through the Fear and Learning Zones to the Growth Zone.

To ensure that growth, coachees must ask themselves, "What's the one thing I'm not doing that would help me grow?" Each of us always has *something*, but we have to identify that one great thing and start working on it. Get it on your schedule. What's the one thing you could be doing now that in two years you will be thanking yourself for? As a coach, you can reinforce their confidence to try something new. It's not about trying something new and then giving up. Whether the coachee passes or fails doesn't matter. What matters is that they stick to the process and commit to that lead measure so that over time they see significant growth because their coach is holding them accountable.

The process of Discovery, Awareness, Focus, Commitment, and Follow-Up is a continuous process. You might need to take your coachee back to square one and start Discovery over again to help them reconfirm the standard, expectations, and goals. Very few people who underperform don't realize they are underperforming. They are aware and they also don't want to have the conversation and be held accountable. The leaders need to step up and say, "Hey, you're underperforming, and I'm committed to working to get you there."

FINAL THOUGHTS

Whether you're a coach or a coachee, following the Radicle Growth program will improve both your work and personal relationships. Researchers have found that effective coaching delivers a 7x return on investment.[38] Moreover, it creates a supportive environment where people *work together* to succeed. The coachee gains confidence and enjoys success, and the coach gets more time back for their own work while earning the satisfaction of helping a colleague improve. The result is always a strong, efficient, and motivated workplace where success—both on the personal and economic levels—is measured and celebrated.

While this book provides you with the tools you need to improve coaching sessions, you may find it advantageous to contact us for more formal training. Our program includes six interactive coaching modules, six comprehensive workbooks, one-on-one coaching sessions, and a coaching certificate when you've completed it.

When coaching is done well, you can significantly influence and accelerate the growth of your team members and the entire team. The Radicle Growth coaching program provides an evolved, holistic approach to coaching that gives leaders everything they need to create a culture for coaching and get team members to take ownership of their own development.

---

38   Jessica Hill Holm, "The 7x ROI of Employee Coaching," *Training*, April 12, 2024, https://trainingmag.com/the-7x-roi-of-employee-coaching/.

CHAPTER 10 GROWTH REFLECTION QUESTIONS AND ACTIVITIES

1. Write down three areas of your life that you could improve by using better questions. Why are those questions going to help?
2. How do you measure success for yourself and others?
   A. How often do you measure your success?
   B. What is your cadence for that personal evaluation?
   C. Are you on track to achieve your personal expectations?
   D. How could you improve your method for measuring your progress?
3. Are you measuring the success of the people you lead as effectively as you are measuring your own success?
4. Final activity: What are the biggest takeaways from this book? Name an area where what you've learned has had the greatest impact on your personal and professional practices. Share your thoughts on our website and read how others are using this method to improve themselves and their relationships.